G. W. BOWERSOCK is Professor of Ancient History,
Institute for Advanced Study, Princeton.

This book examines the historical context of the earliest Christian martyrs, and anchors their grisly and often wilful self-sacrifice to the everyday life and outlook of the cities of the Roman empire.

Professor Bowersock begins by investigating both the time and the region in which martyrdom as we know it came into being. He also offers comparisons of the Graeco-Roman background with the martyrology of Jews and Muslims. A study of official protocols illuminates the bureaucratic institutions of the Roman state as they applied to the first martyrs; and the martyrdoms themselves are seen within the context of urban life (and public spectacle) in the great imperial cities. By considering martyrdom in relation to suicide, the author is also able to demonstrate the peculiarly Roman character of Christian self-sacrifice in relation to other forms of deadly resistance to authority.

THE WILES LECTURES GIVEN AT
THE QUEEN'S UNIVERSITY OF BELFAST

Martyrdom and Rome

MARTYRDOM
AND ROME

G. W. BOWERSOCK

Institute for Advanced Study, Princeton

CAMBRIDGE
UNIVERSITY PRESS

Published by the Press Syndicate of the University of Cambridge
The Pitt Building, Trumpington Street, Cambridge CB2 1RP
40 West 20th Street, New York, NY 10011–4211, USA
10 Stamford Road, Oakleigh, Melbourne 3166, Australia

First published 1995

Printed in Great Britain at the University Press, Cambridge

A catalogue record for this book is available from the British Library

Library of Congress cataloguing in publication data
Bowersock, G. W. (Glen Warren), 1936–
Martyrdom and Rome / G. W. Bowersock.
p.   cm. – (The Wiles lectures given at the Queen's University
of Belfast)
Includes bibliographical references and index.
ISBN 0 521 46539 7 (hardback)
1. Persecution – History – Early church, ca. 30–600.
2. Martyrdom (Christianity) – History of doctrines – Early church, ca. 30–600.
3. Rome – Politics and government – 30 BC–476 AD.
I. Title.   II. Series: Wiles lectures.
BR1604.2.B68   1995
272'.1–dc20   94-28665 CIP

ISBN 0 521 46539 7 hardback

A la chère mémoire
de Louis Robert

Contents

Preface

On four luminous days in May of 1993 I had the honour and the joy of delivering the Wiles Lectures at the Queen's University in Belfast. Before an audience of broad interests and deep intelligence I touched upon the historical context of a phenomenon that had, even as I spoke, a powerful resonance in the political life of Northern Ireland. Martyrdom, I argued, first came into being in the Roman empire and was inextricably rooted in a society and culture peculiar to that world. The later transformation of the concept and the practice of martyrdom lay outside my theme (and my competence), but I know that it was never far from the minds of my listeners.

It is a tradition of the Wiles Lectures that the lecturer meet each evening with university colleagues and invited guests for discussion of the afternoon's lecture. I am immensely indebted to all who contributed to the discussions for their insight, criticism, and benevolence. The late Professor Lewis Warren led each meeting with wisdom and skill. For this and for hospitality of many kinds I remain permanently in his debt. I thank as well those distinguished friends and colleagues who came to Belfast to hear the lectures and participate in the nightly colloquies: David Braund, Averil Cameron, Werner Eck, Edmond Frézouls, Keith Hopkins, Christopher Jones, François Paschoud, David Potter, and Lellia Cracco Ruggini. It was a singularly testing experience to discuss with specialists a set of lectures addressed, in the first instance, to a general audience.

Janet Boyd endowed the Wiles Lectures and graced each of mine with her presence. I hope that *Martyrdom and Rome* may be, in some measure, worthy of her great generosity and vision.

G. W. B.
22 December 1993

I

The making of martyrdom

Towards the end of the reign of the Roman emperor Commodus, in the last years of the decade of the 180s AD, a Roman governor in the province of Asia was conducting his normal judicial activities when a throng of excited people pushed forward to stand before his tribunal. Without provocation or prior accusation they all voluntarily declared themselves to be Christians, and by this declaration they presumably showed themselves unwilling to sacrifice to the Roman emperor – a test to which governors regularly put professing Christians. The pious mob encouraged the governor to do his duty and consign them all promptly to death. He obligingly had a few of them led away to execution; but, as the remainder clamored ever more loudly to be granted the same reward, he cried out to the petitioners in exasperation, "You wretches, if you want to die, you have cliffs to leap from and ropes to hang by."[1] The Roman official, who was a well-known member of a famous senatorial family at Rome, would hardly have confronted Christians for the first time on this occasion. He must have known their enthusiasm for death at the hands of the Roman administration. The philosophic emperor Marcus Aurelius had, not long before, wondered to himself in his *Meditations* why it was that the Christians were

---

[1] Tertull., *ad Scap.* 5. The exasperated proconsul was C. Arrius Antoninus in the reign of Commodus: B. Thomasson, *Laterculi Praesidum* I (Göteborg, 1984), col. 232, no. 162.

so unreasonable and disorderly.[2] Marcus, as a good Stoic, deplored irrational suicide, and he certainly could not comprehend it when others were expected to deliver the fatal blow.

The scene in the province of Asia, an administrative region which corresponds roughly today with the central portion of western Turkey, was recalled by the great patristic writer Tertullian in an address to a Roman governor in North Africa early in the third century. Tertullian eloquently threatened that the scene might be repeated in Carthage:

> If you think that Christians should be persecuted, what will you do with thousands and thousands of men and women of every age and every rank presenting themselves to you? How many fires and how many swords will you need? How will Carthage itself tolerate the decimation of its population at your hands when everyone knows relatives and friends who have been removed, when everyone sees even men and women of your own senatorial order and aristocratic leaders of the city, relatives and friends of your own friends?[3]

The rush to martyrdom was presented by Tertullian as an ever-present danger to the Roman government.

Tertullian himself had, at a stage in his career, imbibed the sentiments of one of the great leaders of an early Christian sect in Asia Minor, a certain Montanus, through whom the Holy Spirit was alleged to have pronounced the following dire injunction: "Desire not to die in bed, in miscarriages, or soft fevers, but in martyrdoms, to glorify Him who suffered for you."[4] Suffering and death at the hands of persecuting magistrates so elevated the status and presumably future prospects of martyrs that, by the late second century, there

---

[2] Marc. Aur., *ad se ipsum* 11.3. Cf. the perplexity of the younger Pliny earlier in the second century, when confronted by Christians who refused to acknowledge the divinity of the Roman emperor: *Epist.* 10.96.

[3] Tertull., *ad Scap.* 5.

[4] On Tertullian's Montanist period, see T. D. Barnes, *Tertullian* (Oxford, 1971), pp. 131–42. For the command of the Holy Spirit, Tertull., *de fuga* 9, *ad fin.*

2

were many Christians (although it is impossible to say just
how many) who actively courted their own deaths as martyrs.
This phenomenon of voluntary martyrdom was by no means
an eccentricity of the period: it continued for more than a
century. The ecclesiastical historian Eusebius reports that he
saw Christians condemned to death in massive numbers in
Upper Egypt in the early fourth century, and he indicates that
most of these were volunteers, who, as soon as one of their
number had been condemned, leapt up one after another
before the judgment seat to confess themselves to be Christians.[5] In Sicily at about the same time another governor was
astonished to hear a man walk past and cry out, "I wish to die,
for I am a Christian." The presiding officer courteously
responded, "Come in, whoever said that. And the blessed
Euplus [for such was his name] entered the courtroom,
bearing the immaculate Gospels." The blessed Euplus's wish
was soon fulfilled.[6]

Voluntary martyrdom astonished the pagans, as well it
might. Marcus Aurelius was not the only thoughtful person of
the age who contemplated with incredulity what he saw
going on around him. Celsus, the author of a highly sophisticated and detailed tract on the Christians, came to the conclusion that the Christians were simply out of their minds –
insane – because they "deliberately" rushed forward to arouse
the anger of an emperor or a governor in order to bring upon
themselves blows, torture, and even death.[7] Half a century
later the Christian apologist Origen attempted to answer this
criticism of Celsus, but he found very little to say because such
conduct was widespread and, in many quarters, admired.[8]

Although Origen claimed that the Christians were doing

---

[5] Euseb., *Hist. Eccles.* 8.9.5.
[6] *Acta Eupli, ad init.* (both Greek and Latin recensions). On voluntary martyrdom,
see G. E. M. de Ste Croix, "Why Were the Early Christians Persecuted?," *Past
and Present* no. 26 (1963), 6–38 (particularly 21–4).
[7] Celsus, *apud* Orig., *contra Cels.* 8.39, 41, 55, 65.   [8] Orig., *contra Cels*, 8.65.

nothing "contrary to the law and word of God," the spread of voluntary martyrdoms had become so alarming to many thoughtful churchmen that they gradually developed a sharp distinction between solicited martyrdom and the more traditional kind that came as a result of persecution. Clement of Alexandria, Origen, Cyprian, and Lactantius, all great spokesmen of the early Church, attempted to stop this enthusiasm and reserve the ranks of the martyrs for those who endured suffering and death in the face of persecution.[9] But the efforts of leading intellectuals and dignitaries did little to stop the enthusiasm. By the end of the fourth century the Christian writer Sulpicius Severus observed wryly that the martyrs of the early Church desired death even more eagerly than clergymen desired a bishopric.[10]

It seems evident that the earliest authentic martyrs suffered torture and death at the hands of Roman officials who were determined to enforce the traditional worship of the Roman emperors and to root out what seemed a seditious new cult.[11] Those martyrs had received much recognition and were believed to have found so great a reward in death that others clearly wanted to emulate them. As Gibbon remarked with a characteristically pungent turn of phrase, "The assurance of a lasting reputation upon earth, a motive so congenial to the vanity of human nature, often served to animate the courage of the martyrs."[12] For true martyrs were forgiven their sins and did indeed acquire a lasting reputation upon earth.

Although voluntary martyrdoms are hardly so common in modern times as they were in the days of the Roman empire, the fact and the concept of martyrdom continue to be a powerful force at the intersection of religion and politics even

---

[9] See, for discussion and reference, G. W. Clarke, *The Letters of St. Cyprian*, vol. 1 (New York, 1984), pp. 303–4.

[10] Sulp. Sev., *Chron.* 2.32.4: ... *multoque avidius tum martyria gloriosis mortibus quaerebantur, quam nunc episcopatus pravis ambitionibus appetuntur.*

[11] See de Ste Croix, "Why were the Early Christians Persecuted?"

[12] E. Gibbon, *Decline and Fall of the Roman Empire*, ch. 16 [vol. 2, p. 110, Bury].

today. Martyrdom was not something that the ancient world had seen from the beginning. What we can observe in the second, third, and fourth centuries of our era is something entirely new. Of course, in earlier ages principled and courageous persons, such as Socrates at Athens or the three Jews in the fiery furnace of Nebuchadnezzar, had provided glorious examples of resistance to tyrannical authority and painful suffering before unjust judges. But never before had such courage been absorbed into a conceptual system of posthumous recognition and anticipated reward, nor had the very word martyrdom existed as the name for this system. Martyrdom, as we understand it, was conceived and devised in response to complex social, religious, and political pressures, and the date and the circumstances of its making are still the subject of lively debate.

"Martyr" is now, after all, a technical term and a powerful one. An honorable or glorious death has nothing like the resonance of martyrdom, which has inspired sophisticated and untutored persons alike to plunge eagerly into the afterlife. "Martyr" is in origin the Greek word μάρτυς, which becomes μάρτυρος, μάρτυρες, in the oblique cases, and this is a word that simply means "witness." It has a long and interesting history in the Greek language from earliest times in that sense. It was naturally part of the legal language of the Greek courts, and it could be used metaphorically for all kinds of observation and attestation.[13] But, until the Christian literature of the mid-second century AD, it had never designated dying for a cause. When it finally assumed that sense, its meaning of "witness" began to slip away, so that the word "martyr" in Greek and the same word borrowed in Latin came more and more to mean what it means today. When Gibbon, in chapter 38 of his *Decline and Fall*, took note that the

---

[13] Cf. for example, B. W. Frier, *American Journal of Legal History* 36 (1992), 389, reviewing P. Cartledge, P. Millett, and S. Todd (eds.), *Nomos: Essays in Athenian Law, Politics, and Society* (Cambridge, 1990).

Catholic Sigismund had acquired the honors of a saint and martyr, he paused to exclaim in a footnote, "A martyr! How strangely that word has been distorted from its original sense of a common witness."[14]

There can be no doubt that among the Christians an intense and seemingly irrational desire to die at the hands of persecutors antedated the creation of the terminology that transformed the common word for "witness." Consider, for example, Ignatius of Antioch in the early second century. He would undoubtedly qualify as a voluntary martyr in terms of his actions. When he was taken from Antioch on the Syrian coast to Rome for execution, he was allowed to stop in Smyrna in Asia Minor. There he communicated with the principal churches of the region, and he wrote a letter to the Christians at Rome begging them not to do anything that would prevent his being given to the wild beasts when he arrived there.[15] He displayed in his writing what has been described as a "pathological yearning for martyrdom."[16] But his language nowhere includes the word. He says that he is in love with death, and he anticipates with joy the tortures that lie ahead: "Come, fire and cross, and encounters with beasts, incisions and dissections, wrenching of bones, hacking of limbs, crushing of the whole body."[17] In one of his most famous metaphors he expressed his hope of being "ground by the teeth of wild beasts" into "the pure bread" of Christ.[18] Yet with all this, Ignatius betrays no knowledge of the language or concept of martyrdom. But he certainly longed for death.

The origins of the phenomenon have long excited scholarly and theological debate. In his book on pagans and Christians, Robin Lane Fox asks (and attempts to answer) the question,

---

[14] E. Gibbon, *Decline and Fall*, ch. 38 [vol. 4, p. 121, Bury].

[15] Ignatius, *Epist. ad Rom.* 5.2 and 8.1–3.

[16] De Ste Croix, "Why were the Early Christians Persecuted?"

[17] Ignatius, *Epist. ad Rom.* 5.3.

[18] Ignatius, *Epist. ad Rom.* 4.1.

"How had this powerful idea of the martyr been constructed?"[19] The new *Oxford History of Christianity* observes, with
admirable restraint, "The Christians called heroes of integrity,
'witnesses,' martyrs. Why this word was specially chosen has
been the subject of scholarly controversy."[20] And that unim-
peachable German repository of classical learning, Pauly-
Wissowa's encyclopaedia, declares in its article on martyrs,
"The origin of this designation continues to be controversial."[21] Thirty years ago a young German theological student
devoted 250 large pages to this subject – very well, I may add –
but in a work that hardly anyone reads because of its
elephantine traversal of the jungle of sources.[22] I am under no
illusion that the subject will be less controversial when I have
finished this chapter, but I dare to hope that its outline and
issues will be clearer.

As the case of Ignatius reminds us, one must consider the
desire for death in conjunction with the concept of martyrdom. But they are not the same. Pathological desire comes
first; but, despite modern claims to the contrary, there is no
reason to think that anyone displayed anything comparable
to martyrdom before the Christians. The only antecedent
parallels that are customarily cited are the death of Socrates at
the very beginning of the fourth century BC and two episodes
in the history of the Maccabees in Palestine during the second
century BC. The story of the fiery furnace had a happy ending
and hardly constitutes anything like martyrdom, despite
claims that it does. Neither the case of Socrates nor that of the
Maccabees demonstrates that the idea of martyrdom should
be attached to earlier societies. I want to argue that martyr-

---

[19] Robin Lane Fox, *Pagans and Christians* (New York, 1987), p. 436.

[20] J. McManners (ed.), *Oxford History of Christianity* (Oxford, 1990), p. 41, from the
experienced pen of Henry Chadwick.

[21] Pauly-Wissowa, *Realencyclopädie der classischen Altertumswissenschaft* 14.2
(Stuttgart, 1930), col. 2044.

[22] Norbert Brox, *Zeuge und Märtyrer: Untersuchungen zur frühchristlichen Zeugnis-
Terminologie* (Munich, 1961).

dom was alien to both the Greeks and the Jews, and the position I take here is close to that of Delehaye and von Campenhausen among the many scholars who have discussed this subject.[23]

Socrates certainly is, in the modern sense, one of the greatest martyrs of western civilization; but, if we apply the word "martyr" to him, it is only retrospectively with full knowledge of what a real martyr was like. Socrates was courageous, holding to his principles in the face of unjust condemnation, and he hoped (but was certainly not sure) that things might be better after he drank the hemlock. A real martyr knows that things will be better, at least for him or for her. Let us recall, for example, the magnificent ending of the *Apology* of Socrates, as Plato has recreated it for us:

> But you, men of the jury, must be of good hope when it comes to the matter of death. Consider this one point to be true – that a good man cannot suffer evil either when alive or when dead and that his affairs are not neglected by the gods. Whereas what has happened to me occurred by accident, this much is clear to me: that it is better for me to die and to be set free from these troubles.

The *Apology* goes on to conclude with the celebrated words, "Now it is time to go away, for me to die and for you to live. Which of us will have the better fate is unclear to everyone except to god."[24]

It is perfectly true that, for a time in the history of the early Christian Church, Socrates was mentioned as a kind of pre-Christian martyr, although eventually the Church deplored such citations of non-Christian examples, and of Socrates in

---

23 H. Delehaye, *Les passions des martyrs et les genres littéraires* (Brussels, 1921); H. von Campenhausen, *Die Idee des Martyriums in der alten Kirche* (Göttingen, 1936). For an altogether different perspective, see T. Baumeister, *Die Anfänge der Theologie des Martyriums* (Münster, 1980). A useful survey of recent literature on the theology and origins of martyrdom appears in Boudewijn Dehandschutter, *Aufstieg und Niedergang der röm. Welt* II.27.1 (1993), pp. 508–14.

24 Plato, *Apol.* 41c–42a.

particular.[25] The recorded martyrdoms of Apollonius in the second century and Pionios in the third both cite Socrates as an example,[26] but it is fair to say that these allusions occur in the context of persuading incredulous pagans that what the martyrs are doing is not irrational. It is a rhetorical argument and admittedly one of considerable force. It does not constitute a statement that Socrates was, in the Christian sense, a martyr. And, needless to say, Socrates nowhere speaks of himself as a martyr, nor does anyone else. The word turns up in the *Apology* only in its proper sense of "witness" in order to affirm that the god Apollo at Delphi can attest to the wisdom of Socrates. "He, the god," says Socrates, "is the witness I shall give you."[27] It is obviously an elevated form of the purely judicial use of the word.

The so-called martyrdoms in the history of the Maccabees are another matter altogether. In many treatments of this problem they have served as the basis for ascribing the whole concept of martyrdom to the Jews. Both Christians and Jews in late antiquity and the Middle Ages considered the episodes of courage in the Books of the Maccabees as examples of martyrdom. But they are not described as such there. More important, the whole concept of martyrdom in Judaism, as expressed by the phrase *qiddus̆ ha-shem* (sanctification of the name), does not occur until after the Tannaitic period – not until late antiquity at the earliest.[28] The alleged martyrdoms at Masada in the first century or of Rabbi Akiva in the second are all retrospective constructions of a posterior age, an age sub-

---

[25] G. M. A. Hanfmann, "Socrates and Christ," *Harvard Studies in Classical Philology* 60 (1951), 205–33; K. Döring, *Exemplum Socratis* (Wiesbaden, 1979), ch. 7: "Das Beispiel des Socrates bei den frühchristlichen Märtyrern und Apologeten," pp. 143–61. Also see G. W. Clarke, *The Octavius of Marcus Minucius Felix* (New York, 1974), pp. 240–1.

[26] *Mart. Pionii* 17; *Acta Apollonii* 41.   [27] Plato, *Apol.* 20e.

[28] S. Safrai, "Martyrdom in the Teachings of the Tannaim," in T. C. de Kruijf, H.v.d. Sandt, *Sjaloom* (Arnhem, 1983), pp. 145–64. On the whole subject, see J. W. van Henten (ed.), *Die Entstehung der jüdischen Martyrologie* (Leiden, 1989).

stantially later than that of the first Christian martyrdoms. Now let us look at the Maccabean episodes in detail.

Among the books of the Biblical Apocrypha is a moving account of the resistance of the Maccabees to the strenuous efforts of the Seleucid monarch Antiochus IV to force Jews into a Hellenic way of life. These struggles took place a little before the middle of the second century BC. What we now possess are abbreviated versions, known as epitomes, of an allegedly longer account that is lost. In the so-called second book of Maccabees, two powerful stories are told of resistance to the royal order that Jews should eat pork.[29] These two stories are absent from the account in the first book of Maccabees, and there is good reason, both textual and historical, to believe (as most scholars now do) that at least the second story is a later insertion into the narrative given in the second book of Maccabees. It is possible that the first is an addition as well. In a work that celebrates in almost every chapter the Second Temple at Jerusalem (destroyed in AD 70) as still standing, doubtless reflecting an obsession of the longer original text, the two tales of resistance utterly lack any reference to the Temple. And the second tale puts the Seleucid king in Palestine when he was not there.

Both of these intrusive stories received dramatically amplified treatment at an unknown date in the work that we know today as the fourth book of Maccabees. There can be no doubt that this latter work was written under the Roman empire. Although current opinion puts the second book a century or more earlier,[30] it could equally be of Roman imperial date (although before 70). It is often forgotten that the first allusion to the extant books of the Maccabees does not appear until the writings of Clement of Alexandria in the late second century.[31]

---

[29] II Macc. 6–7.
[30] Cf. Chr. Habicht, 2. *Makkabäerbuch, Jüdische Schriften aus hellenistisch-römischer Zeit*, vol. 1 (Gütersloh, 1976).
[31] Clem. Alex., *Strom.* 5.14.97 (ἡ τῶν Μακκαβαίων ἐπιτομή).

The stunning resemblance of the resistance shown in the two stories of the second and fourth books to the resistance shown in various Christian martyrdoms has led many to believe that these accounts reveal a Jewish tradition that surfaced here to provide the inspiration and model for what came later. Certainly one can readily admit that they were a primary justification for including books of the Maccabees in the Biblical Apocrypha, and they were undoubtedly much appreciated by the apologists of the early Church. But since there is no reason to think that the two accounts reflect the historical time of the Maccabees, what time they do reflect is anyone's guess. Inasmuch as they do not make reference to the Temple and seem to be additions to the narrative, they could even be associated with the Roman empire after AD 70.

The first story concerns the aged Eleazer, who refused to eat pork and refused equally to engage in a subterfuge proposed by his friends and well-wishers to extricate him from the difficult situation in which he found himself. He stood by his principles with courage and eloquence. He declared that, if he escaped the punishment of man, he would then be subject to the punishment of the Lord, which he could escape neither in life nor in death. The author of Second Maccabees said that he preferred death with glory to life with pollution, and consequently he went voluntarily (αὐθαιρέτως in Greek) to the execution block. At the end of his narration the author observes that he left behind an example of nobility and a reminder of virtue for generations to come. Nowhere in the Greek of Second Maccabees (nor in the considerably more elaborate account in Fourth Maccabees) does the word "martyr" appear. Eleazer is presented as a shining example of death with glory (ὁ μετὰ εὐκλείας θάνατος),[32] a death as old as the *Iliad*.

The second story carries an even greater impact because it

---

[32] II Macc. 6.19.

involves an entire family – a mother with her seven children. Each of the children in turn refuses to cooperate with the royal order and goes to his death. Finally the mother herself ends her life after her children. This powerful narration is, like the account of Eleazer, vastly amplified in the fourth book of Maccabees. But again the word "martyrdom" does not appear, although in one passage in the later Fourth Maccabees διαμαρτυρία is used in a conventional judicial sense.[33] Protestations of the sons and what the author of Second Maccabees calls "the excessive torments" they suffered inevitably recall the Martyr Acts and constitute a parallel to them. The question is, quite simply, whether or not the accounts of Eleazer and the mother with her sons antedate the concept of martyrdom as it was shaped by the Christians.

As we have seen, no one believes that any of the books of the Maccabees are actually contemporaneous with the events they describe. If the narratives of Eleazer and the mother with her sons are insertions into the second book of Maccabees by the epitomator (or subsequently by someone else), there is no indication that these two stories must belong before the middle of the first century AD. The only thing of which we can be certain is that the narratives in the second book of Maccabees must precede the more amplified versions in the fourth, which could have been composed at any time down to Clement of Alexandria. This leaves us with a possible date for the stories of Eleazer and the mother with her sons in the second half of the first century, in other words, in the time when the New Testament documents were coming into being and the zealous Ignatius was growing up.

This was the time in which we first glimpse, in a chronologically secure context, the new concept of martyrdom, although still without the word. So if the two stories in the books of the Maccabees have nothing to do either with the

---

[33] IV Macc. 16.16.

authentic history of the Maccabees or with the lost original text that recounted it, it may be suggested that they have everything to do with the aspirations and literature of the early Christians. There are some indications that the Greek text of the story of the mother with her sons in Second Maccabees was translated from a Hebrew or Aramaic original.[34] This intimation of a Semitic source for the heroic tales that the Christians soon absorbed into their own tradition makes it reasonable to suggest that they arose in the world of mid first-century Palestine or slightly later.

Consideration of the so-called Maccabean martyrs brings us, therefore, precisely to the period and language of the New Testament. It is through the texts preserved there that we must look for possible allusions to the idea and terminology of martyrdom. The earliest appearance of the words "martyr" and "martyrdom" in the clear sense of death at the hands of hostile secular authority is the martyrdom of Polycarp in Asia (western Asia Minor) in about 150. The narrator says:

> We are writing to you, dear brothers, the story of the martyrs and of blessed Polycarp who put a stop to the persecution by his own martyrdom [διὰ τῆς μαρτυρίας] as though he were putting a seal upon it ... Blessed indeed and noble are all the martyrdoms that took place in accordance with God's will ... For even when [the martyrs] were torn by whips until the very structure of their bodies was laid bare down to the inner veins and arteries, they endured it, making even the bystanders weep for pity.[35]

The account of Polycarp's martyrdom is not likely to have been written very much after the event. Accordingly it looks as if the concept of martyrdom was constructed by the Christians in the hundred years or so between about 50 and 150, and the word adapted in the second half of that period. The coincidence with the composition of the New Testament would suggest that the stories of Jesus's life and death were ◆

---

[34] Cf. Habicht, 2. *Makkabäerbuch* (n. 30 above), p. 171.   [35] *Mart. Polycarpi* 2.

related in one way or another to this extraordinary development.

The Greek word μάρτυς appears frequently in the New Testament, but nowhere can it be shown without question to be used in any sense other than that of "witness."[36] In the Gospels and particularly in the Acts of the Apostles, the word is used to designate those who witnessed Jesus's suffering and those who witnessed his resurrection. Hence the word is in many cases simply another way of describing an apostle. In the Apocalypse (the book of Revelation) Jesus himself appears as a faithful witness (ὁ μάρτυς ὁ πιστός), a striking phrase that may even reflect John's deep knowledge of classical Greek since that expression can be traced back to the poet Pindar.[37] It is obvious that Jesus bore witness to the glory of God, and there is nothing to suggest here that John refers to him as a martyr who died at the hands of the Roman authorities.

There are only two passages in the entire text of the Greek New Testament that could conceivably be interpreted as using the word μάρτυς in the new sense of martyr. But the improbability of such a use even in these instances is underscored by the many cases in the New Testament in which the word means simply "witness." Nonetheless, these two passages could have provided a solid foundation for any subsequent redefinition of the word. Both involve persons who were put to death. Hence the ambiguity of their being described as μάρτυς. John, in the second chapter of the Apocalypse, makes reference to an otherwise unknown Antipas whom he describes, curiously, in the same words that he actually uses for Jesus himself, "a faithful witness," in this case qualified with the possessive "my faithful witness": "Antipas was my faithful μάρτυς [witness], who was slain

---

[36] Cf. W. Bauer, K. and B. Aland, *Wörterbuch zum Neuen Testament*, 6th edn (Berlin, 1988), s.v. μάρτυς, cols. 1001–2.

[37] Apoc. 1.5, 3.14. Cf. Pind., *Pyth.* 1.88.

among you."[38] He was not a μάρτυς *because* he was slain, but a witness who was slain.

The other case is better known and more amply described in the New Testament: it is the story of Stephen, stoned to death after delivering an eloquent speech in response to an accusation of blasphemy. The speech concludes with Stephen's literally bearing witness, as he declares that he sees the heavens opening before him and Jesus standing on the right hand of God. At this point his audience "cried out with a loud voice, and stopped their ears, and ran upon him with one accord, and cast him out of the city, and stoned him."[39] Later in the book of Acts Paul alludes to the stoning of Stephen by the words, "When the blood of your martyr Stephen was shed."[40] Only a few verses earlier Paul had referred to God's choice of himself as "a witness to all men" of what he had seen and heard,[41] and so it is hard to believe that in his reference to Stephen, almost immediately after, the sense of witness would be any more loaded than it was in the reference he made to himself. Stephen was a witness of the glory of the Lord and could legitimately be called "your witness." On the other hand, since he did suffer a violent death (albeit at the hands of his fellow Jews) and the shedding of his blood is linked to his being called witness, his witnessing could obviously be construed as consisting in that death. This, in my view, is the one passage in the entire New Testament that might have effectively encouraged the sense of martyrdom as it was to develop. The allusion to Antipas could then have been construed in a similar way.

We have already observed that, when Ignatius was craving to be burned, eaten, and ground up into the pure bread of Christ, he never once availed himself of the term "martyr," and he was certainly writing after the composition of the Acts.

---

[38] Apoc. 2.13.   [39] Acta Apost. 7.56–8.
[40] Acta Apost. 22.20: ὅτε ἐξεχύννετο τὸ αἷμα Στεφάνου τοῦ μάρτυρός σου.
[41] Acta Apost. 22.15: μάρτυς . . . πρὸς πάντας ἀνθρώπους.

His example suggests that, although the sacrifice and death that we associate with martyrdom was already appreciated and sought after, it had not yet received a name. The example of Jesus himself, to say nothing of Stephen, Antipas, and others, must surely have constituted the ultimate background for the development of aspirations such as those of Ignatius. It is worth comparing parallel developments in secular history of the same period (the second half of the first century). This was an age in which philosophers as well as Christians stood up to the tyrannical authority of Rome and its emperor, even to the point of exile and death. Their resistance, documented in traditional classical texts as well as modern discoveries on papyrus, shows a spreading desire for liberty and for freedom from the oppressor that, in those terms, has a deep and memorable history across the centuries and particularly in the Old Testament. None of these *Acts of the Pagan Martyrs*, as some of these narratives have been called, has the characteristics of Christian martyrdom except insofar as they oppose the ruling authority.[42] The Stoics were particularly famous for resisting the emperor, and a well-known group of Stoic philosophers at Rome earned everlasting fame for their outspoken resistance.[43] Nor were the Stoics alone in this. The fabulous wonder-worker, Apollonius of Tyana, was a Pythagorean, who showed no less courage, it seems, before the tyrant Domitian.[44]

Early in the second century the philosopher Epictetus in his *Dissertations* proclaimed that the philosopher was called by Zeus to be his witness. The language of Epictetus has long been seen to provide an interesting parallel with the language of the New Testament. Zeus sends evil to test men, and he uses philosophers to instruct them, says Epictetus: "The philo-

---

[42] Cf. H. Musurillo, *Acts of the Pagan Martyrs* (Oxford, 1954).

[43] See Ch. Wirszubski, *Libertas as a Political Idea at Rome during the Late Republic and Early Principate* (Cambridge, 1960).

[44] Philostr., *Vit. Apoll.* 7.32–4.

sophers are the witnesses for the uneducated."[45] They are also, according to Epictetus, the witnesses of those matters in which mortal man has no choice. "The philosopher is, for the benefit of others," says Epictetus, "a witness [the word is *martyr*] of those things that cannot be chosen."[46] In another remarkable passage the philosopher is described simply as "a martyr called by God"[47] – martyr here clearly in the sense of "witness" but allowing, even in this polytheist context, a sense of mission that resembles, although in a far less sanguinary way, the self-perception of Ignatius.

In these early years of the second century, in both the polytheist and Christian contexts and also, I suspect (on the basis of my interpretation of Second Maccabees), the Palestinian Jewish context, the concept of martyrdom as we know it gradually took shape. With it soon came the word "martyrdom" among the Christians in its modern sense. If the martyrdom of Polycarp is the first attested example of word and act together, obviously it need not have been the first. The subsequent early examples of martyrs, however, seem often to come from Asia Minor (the martyrdoms of Polycarp, Pionios, and all those voluntary martyrs before the governor mentioned by Tertullian). Even Ignatius, who sounds so much like a martyr, wrote his fiery letters in the bosom of the Christian churches of Asia Minor. One cannot help wondering therefore whether or not this invention of martyrdom had some kind of root in western Asia Minor, that is to say Anatolia – the part of the Roman empire in which it first and repeatedly appeared. Even the martyrs of Lyon in 177, going to their deaths far away in France, were in close touch with their brethren in Anatolia. Our knowledge of their martyrdoms comes from a letter they wrote to the churches of Asia and Phrygia (a region within western Asia Minor).[48]

The Asian, or more precisely the Anatolian connection,

---

[45] Epict., *Diss.* 3.26, 28. [46] Epict., *Diss.* 3.24, 112: μάρτυρα τῶν ἀπροαιρέτων.
[47] Epict., *Diss.* 1.29, 47. [48] *Mart. Lugdun.*, ad init.

seems to be reflected in the preaching of Montanus, which we have already heard: it is better to die the martyr's death than to die in one's bed, in childbirth, in sickness, or in any other more natural way. It can hardly be an accident that this kind of preaching was carried out in the very area in which martyrdom proved to be so popular. But more than that – Asia Minor was unusually fond of spectacles and public entertainments. It was one of the major training areas for gladiators, and many of the great cities of the region had extravagant provisions for gladiatorial shows and the display of wild animals.[49] Pressure on the part of local authorities to find victims over and above the criminals who would normally be provided for a show must have been unusually great. Various forms of torment to which Christian martyrs were subjected, as we hear of them from Tertullian and other writers, fit perfectly within the framework of those popular entertainments which have been described recently by an outstanding young scholar as "fatal charades."[50] The criminals, or martyrs, would be dressed up as mythological characters and asked to enact bloody roles that would culminate in their real death in some titillatingly gruesome way. The popularity of these fatal charades was hardly peculiar to Asia Minor, but it was certainly conspicuous there.

As we saw at the beginning, martyrdom soon spread. In North Africa early in the third century Tertullian confronted the issue with eloquence and an abundance of examples. By the time of Cyprian in the middle of the third century, the Church had already begun a vigorous effort to discourage voluntary martyrdoms and reserve the martyr's crown for those whose faith was truly tested by the secular authority.[51]

[49] Louis Robert, *Les gladiateurs dans l'Orient grec* (Paris, 1940). There was a training school for gladiators at Pergamum, where the young Galen was able to sharpen his medical skills by direct observation and treatment: Galen 13.599 ff. and 18B, 567 (Kühn).

[50] Kathleen M. Coleman, "Fatal Charades: Roman Executions Staged as Mythological Enactments," *JRS* 80 (1990), 44–73.

[51] G. W. Clarke, *Letters*.

But the discouragement of ineffectual martyrdoms only served to confirm the sense of real ones. The word "martyr" was now securely established in its new meaning. It was soon taken over into other languages, as, for example, a loan word in Latin. It was never *translated* into Latin as *testis*. In Syriac, by contrast, it was translated: the word for "witness" was given the new meaning of "martyr" by reference to the Greek use.

Perhaps the most astonishing and influential extension of the concept of martyrdom as witnessing came in Arabic after the Muslim conquest of Palestine in the seventh century. Just as the Syriac speakers had done, the Arabs translated the Greek word as "witness" into Arabic (*shahîd*). This was to become a designation of Muslim martyrs who fell in battle before the infidel and could therefore count on great rewards in the afterlife. The Islamic concept of martyrdom has had far-reaching consequences, as everyone who reads the news-papers today will know. The terrorists who blew up American soldiers in Beirut are martyrs. The Iraqis who died in the invasion of Kuwait are martyrs. There can be little doubt that this concept – and this word – was absorbed directly from Greek during those early centuries of Islam when Christian churches still flourished in Palestine and Greek was still spoken.

Arab theologians were confronted by a curious dilemma in interpreting the word for "witness," *shahîd*, because the form, unlike the Greek equivalent (or indeed the Syriac one), is a passive form and can therefore also mean "witnessed." The Arabs had accordingly to confront the awkward question of whether a martyr was witnessing, and if so what or whom, or whether he was witnessed by another. If the word was to be understood as "being witnessed" rather than "witnessing," then the witness could only be God Himself (or His angels), and hence the occasional interpretation of the Islamic martyr as a person whose death was witnessed by God or the angels.[52] Such an interpretation brings us, in a curious way, full circle to the death of Socrates, for Socrates too claimed that he was witnessed by god – it was Apollo, you will recall, that bore witness to him, although in life not in death.

The structure of the language of Islam made the notion of martyrdom rather more complex than it was in its original Christian form. In popular contexts it was even extended to the deaths of pious Muslims on the pilgrimage route to Mecca. Many travelers have observed that the graves of pilgrims often identified them as, in Arabic, "martyrs" (*shuhûd*). This point was of sufficient interest to that crusty but indomitable traveler, Charles Doughty, that he remarked in his *Travels in Arabia Deserta*, "Many are the hasty graves of buried pilgrim 'witnesses' in this station; upon the headstones of wild blocks pious friends have scored the words which were their names. To be accounted 'witnessing,' surely for civil souls, is the creeping plague of Egypt."[53]

By contrast, the effort of the young Christian Church to reduce the enthusiasm for martyrdom that had caused some embarrassment in the early centuries seems generally to have been successful and to have left martyrdom for those who earned it. But human history is never, unfortunately, free from oppression, tyranny, and cruelty. Tertullian had once declared to a Roman governor, "Your cruelty is our glory."[54] And that would seem to be a human predicament that has no end. Martyrdom as it was invented and martyrdom as it is now understood is as powerful a force in the Church that created it as it is in Islam, though obviously in a different way.

When the German theologian Dietrich Bonhöffer was executed at Flossenburg on 9 April 1945, the removal of this good and courageous man at a time when the war was near its end

[52] See the citations marshalled by E. W. Lane, *An Arabic-English Lexicon* (London, 1872), 1.4, p. 1610.

[53] C. Doughty, *Travels in Arabia Deserta*, 3rd edn (New York, 1921), p. 77.

[54] Tertull., *ad Scap.* 5: *crudelitas vestra gloria est nostra.*

has moved many an observer to speak of martyrdom. One such was the poet W. H. Auden, who, a little over a decade later, wrote a poem in memory of Bonhöffer, whom he described in the title as "Martyred at Flossenburg."[55] Some verses from this poem encapsulate better than any prose what lay behind the making of martyrdom:

> What reverence is rightly paid
> To a Divinity so odd
> He lets the Adam whom He made
> Perform the Acts of God? ...
>
> Now, did He really break the seal
> And rise again? We dare not say;
> But conscious unbelievers feel
> Quite sure of Judgment Day.
>
> Meanwhile, a silence on the cross,
> As dead as we shall ever be,
> Speaks of some total gain or loss,
> And you and I are free
>
> To guess from the insulted face
> Just what Appearances He saves
> By suffering in a public place
> A death reserved for slaves.

[55] W. H. Auden, *Collected Poems* (New York, 1976), pp. 509–10.

II
The written record

In the first poem of his anthology of lyrics on the crowns of martyrdom (*Peristephanon Liber*), the Christian Latin poet Prudentius finds that his zeal for recounting the excruciating tortures suffered by the martyrs is severely limited by the loss of records about them. "Alas," he exclaimed, "for the all too common forgetfulness of the voiceless past [*o vetustatis silentis obsoleta oblivio*]!"[1] When we are denied the details, the story itself may be extinguished. Long ago, according to Prudentius, a blasphemous soldier took away the records of martyrs so that subsequent generations, trained in the preservation of memory by written account, should not disseminate to posterity, in sweet language, "the order, time, and manner that was handed down about the martyrdom."[2]

The fundamental written texts, what Prudentius called the *tenaces libelli*,[3] obviously contained the raw material for those inspiring stories of martyrdoms that circulated in the Roman empire from the middle of the second century onwards and perhaps even earlier. These were texts that were adapted, expanded, altered, and imitated throughout the Roman imperial and Byzantine periods. Since the formative period of martyrdom was over by the early fourth century, when the empire became Christian, there could be no more documents of the struggles of the early Church against an intolerant and polytheist bureaucracy. The golden age of Martyr Acts was

[1] Prudentius, *Peristeph.* 1.73.   [2] Prudentius, *Peristeph.* 1.77.
[3] Prudentius, *Peristeph.* 1.76.

not to come again, even though the Church could go on registering new martyrs down to the present time. Imagination and rhetoric could fill in gaps for the early centuries, but even so prolific and rhapsodic a writer as Prudentius knew that his account was ultimately at the mercy of those who, like the blasphemous soldier, chose to destroy the written record.

Whatever authentic memorials survived of the martyrdoms of the pre-Constantinian empire – these were precisely those martyrdoms suffered by Christians who refused to sacrifice to the Roman emperors – served as the basis for all subsequent accounts of the martyrdoms of that period and provided the inspiration for new martyrs whose faith was to be tested in the centuries to follow. The miracles of endurance and fidelity that characterize the Martyr Acts of the Roman imperial period also inspired those hagiographers who recorded the lives of saints with such loving detail. Martyrology and hagiography constitute a twin literary offspring of early Christianity, as opposed to homiletics, exegesis, or epistolography.

The personal sufferings of martyrs and saints created a wholly new literature that was as exciting to read as it was edifying. This literature passed back and forth easily across the frontier between fiction and history, and it acquired its impact from the apparent historicity of its details. It can hardly be accidental, and has often been remarked, that the decline of historical fiction in the Roman empire (the Greek novels in particular) coincided quite precisely with the rise of Martyr Acts. Even if (as I believe) Heliodorus's novel, the *Aethiopica*, represents a return to the novel genre in the later fourth century – perhaps even inspired by the polytheist revival under Julian – the enthusiasm was short-lived and almost immediately followed by a burst of creativity in hagiography. The transitional work in the whole evolution from fiction to martyrology and hagiography is certainly, among the texts that survive, the so-called *Clementine Recognitions*. This bizarre work is nothing less than a piece of historical fiction, much on the lines of the Greek novels we possess, but with a Christian hero and an abundance of inspiring Christian homilies in place of the rhetorical speeches of pagan fiction.[4]

The early Martyr Acts are, therefore, potentially important documents for the taste and nature of Christianity when Rome still had its empire and empowered its far-flung bureaucracy to process recalcitrant Christians within the legal system of the age. This was a world that was manifestly very different from the post-Constantinian one, with a capital in Byzantium as well as in Rome, and with much of the sufferings of Christians inflicted by other Christians. Doctrinal disputes and heresies subsequently provided the fuel for violence in an empire that was no longer administered by pagans. This is not the place to resume the knotty problem of the stages of Roman imperial legislation against Christianity.[5] It will suffice to state the obvious: some emperors and some bureaucrats were more zealous in prosecuting Christians than others, and hence there was an irregular rhythm in the outbreaks of persecution. But one thing is clear, and that is that a Christian who refused to sacrifice to the emperor when called upon to do so was in violation of the law and subject to the extreme penalty. Inevitably all those who became martyrs refused to make such a sacrifice and persisted defiantly to confess their Christian faith. The severity of their punishments depended to some extent upon their status, the bloodthirstiness of the magistrate in charge, and the interests of the community in providing public entertainments. Those who became martyrs were united in refusing the sacrifice test and in persisting openly to confess their Christianity.

The Acts of the early martyrs that we possess clearly contain

---

[4] On the subject of secular fiction in relation to Christian literature, see G. W. Bowersock, *Fiction as History: Nero to Julian*, Sather Lectures (California, 1994). The present Wiles Lectures may be considered as a kind of pendant to the Sather Lectures.

[5] For a survey of the evidence and issues, W. H. C. Frend, *Martyrdom and Persecution in the Early Church* (Blackwell, 1965).

much that is fictional and was introduced by subsequent redactors. But equally clearly these Acts contain much authentic material excerpted and included by the redactors, if occasionally supplemented or altered. In combining fictional elaboration with historical substance, the Martyr Acts bear a relation to the historical events of the time not unlike that of the Gospels. I have argued elsewhere that the historical narratives of the Gospels provided a powerful stimulus to the production of pagan historical fiction.[6] In turn, with the passage of time, the production and popularity of that fiction itself provided an equally powerful stimulus to the composition and dissemination of the Martyr Acts. The mediating role of secular fiction between the Gospels and the Martyr Acts (to say nothing of later hagiography) is guaranteed, it may be argued, by the narrative technique, especially in the handling of circumstantial detail, that characterizes those Acts. Even the literary style of the Martyr Acts is far closer to secular fiction in Greek than it is to the style of the Gospel narratives. The Gospels were products of Hellenized Judaism in Palestine in the late first century, whereas the Martyr Acts are quite palpably the product of the non-Jewish Graeco-Roman society of Asia Minor, Greece, and North Africa.

But the purely literary features of early Christian martyrology hold little or no promise for the historian, and in my view generations of scholars have labored abortively to trace literary motifs that could be paralleled in other texts such as the Old Testament (Daniel, in particular) and the second and fourth books of Maccabees. Perler in 1949,[7] Frend in 1965,[8] and most recently Baumeister in 1980[9] have practiced a kind of crude and antiquated literary criticism to emphasize banal

[6] *Fiction as History.*
[7] O. Perler, "Das vierte Makkabäerbuch, Ignatius von Antiochien und die ältesten Märtyrerakten," *Revista di archeologia cristiana*, 25 (1949), 47–72.
[8] Frend, *Martyrdom.*
[9] T. Baumeister, *Die Anfänge der Theologie des Martyriums* (Münster, 1980).

coincidences in various narratives of resistance to authority and heroic self-sacrifice as if every such episode constituted martyrdom. By these critical procedures Baumeister and his predecessors imagined that they could uncover a dependence, on the part of the authors of martyr acts, upon Jewish sources. But as an acute participant in a colloquium in 1984 on Jewish martyrology observed, "In Christian martyr acts, despite all the differences in form, the kernel is the authentic documentation of the legal hearing. That is perhaps the real difference from Jewish martyr acts, and accordingly the concept of μάρτυς should be understood as a typically Christian title."[10]

The documentary sources for some of the most important early martyrdoms can be discovered in the surviving acts and directly related to the historical world of the martyrs themselves. The written record as it has come down to us contains essentially three forms of documentary account: 1) alleged writings of the martyrs themselves from the days leading up to their martyrdom (writings which, for obvious reasons, did not include the actual moment of execution); 2) eyewitness accounts, in which a sympathetic viewer has recorded his impressions relatively soon after the martyrdom (these accounts invariably supplement what the martyr was unable to supply, notably the death scene); and 3) apparently official transcripts of the proceedings in which the martyr was interrogated before a Roman magistrate. Such transcripts would normally include the judicial decision to punish and the character of the punishment but omit the execution itself. Several of the most important martyrdoms, such as those of Pionios and Perpetua, seem to include testimony from all three types of documentary source. The fabrication of transcripts – or rather the creation of interrogations in the form of an official transcript – certainly cannot be ruled out in some cases, but a

[10] J. W. den Boeft in J. W. van Henten, *Die Entstehung der jüdischen Martyrologie* (Leiden, 1989), p. 221.

demonstrable fabrication of writings of the martyrs themselves or of eyewitness accounts in the first person is less evident and may well not have taken place at all. In general, the disengagement of these three forms of documents leads to a reasonable assessment of the historical value of the Martyr Acts and, in many cases, can be tested against the evidence of inscriptions and papyri that treat of similar administrative and social contexts.

The documentary evidence embedded within the written record accordingly allows the historian to integrate the martyrdoms within the larger fabric of society and administration in the Roman empire. What emerges strikingly from an examination of this material is that the martyrdoms form a cohesive part of the structure of the Roman empire – both bureaucratic and social – and not simply a disconcerting obstruction to the smooth functioning of the imperial government. To put this in another way, Christianity owed its martyrs to the *mores* and structure of the Roman empire, not to the indigenous character of the Semitic Near East where Christianity was born. The written record suggests that, like the very word "martyr" itself, martyrdom had nothing to do with Judaism or with Palestine. It had everything to do with the Graeco-Roman world, its traditions, its language, and its cultural tastes.

This point can best be demonstrated from a selective review of the material in each of the three classes of documentary evidence within the Acts of the martyrs. If, then, we turn first to the texts supposedly left behind by martyrs themselves, we find, in particular, three ample and famous records. These are the *mémoire* that Pionios is said to have written while in prison awaiting execution at Smyrna, the journal kept by Perpetua before her martyrdom at Carthage, and the concomitant diary of a certain Saturus, also evidently composed at the time of the martyrdom of Perpetua.

The first chapter of the surviving *Martyrdom of Pionios* tells us that Pionios left a σύγγραμμα "for our instruction, so that we might have it even now as a memorial of his teaching."[11] It is generally assumed that this σύγγραμμα constituted the basis for the surviving account down to the moment at which Pionios was sent to his death. The narrative, as we have it, is written in the third person, and yet there seem to be one or two moments in which the editor appears to have incorporated the actual references of Pionios to himself and his comrades in the first person plural. The most powerful example concerns an apostate priest, Euctemon, used as an example by the Roman authorities to persuade Pionios to sacrifice. Euctemon tried to force "us," says the text, to eat of the meat of a small lamb brought to the shrine of the two Nemeseis in Smyrna.[12] "Us" here may be the same first person plural that makes an appearance earlier in the martyrdom, when another apostate, a person by the name of Asclepiades, is referred to as being "with us."[13]

It is probably not accidental that these two striking, even surprising, references to Christian apostates who are prepared to sacrifice to the emperor both occur in language that suggests the original text of Pionios himself. Pionios in the third century was clearly not averse to mentioning renegades from his flock, whereas later martyrologists notoriously preferred to suppress information of this kind. The translators of the *Martyrdom of Pionios* into Armenian, Old Church Slavonic, and Latin all, to a greater or lesser extent, cut back on this information or eliminated it altogether.[14]

It is not only in the matter of apostasy that Pionios's account takes us back to a recognizably imperial context. In both of the great speeches that are assigned to him in the martyrdom narrative, he addressed the Jews of Smyrna, a community we

---

[11] *Mart. Pionii* 1.2. Cf. L. Robert, *Le martyre de Pionios*, ed. G. W. Bowersock and C. P. Jones (Dumbarton Oaks, 1994), pp. 49–50.

[12] *Mart. Pionii* 18.13.   [13] *Mart. Pionii* 10.5.

[14] Cf. Robert *Martyre*, pp. 11–12.

know to have been substantial in the second and third centuries.[15] Pionios shows more than a trace of that anti-Semitism
so conspicuous in the account of the martyrdom of Polycarp,
but Pionios is more of a teacher and attempts to make his case
for Christianity in terms that his Jewish listeners would
understand. Like the sophists, to whom Pionios as an orator
may be compared for subtlety and eloquence, he turns the
taunts of Jewish critics back on themselves.

> Who forced the Jews to sacrifice to Beelphagor, or partake of the
> sacrifices offered to the dead, or to fornicate with the daughters of
> foreigners, or to sacrifice their sons and daughters to idols, to
> murmur against God, to slander Moses, to be ungrateful to their
> benefactors, or in their hearts to return to Egypt, or, as Moses went
> up to receive the law, to say to Aaron, "Make gods for us," and
> then to make the calf – and all the other things they did, for they
> are capable of deceiving you. Then let them read to you the Book
> of Judges, Kings, or Exodus, or all the other passages which prove
> them wrong.[16]

This is strong stuff. It is solidly grounded in the tradition of
anti-Jewish literature of the Christian Church. This is the
literature that is conventionally referred to today as *adversus
Iudaeos*, but there it has a directness and intensity, as well as a
rhetorical brilliance, that anchors Pionios's speech securely in
the society of second- and third-century Smyrna.

In his second speech Pionios returns to the attack. He tells
the polytheists of Smyrna not to succumb to the proselytizing
efforts of Jews who invite them to their synagogues. "Do not
become with them rulers of Sodom and people of Gomorrah,
whose hands are tainted with blood. We did not slay our
prophets, nor did we betray Christ and crucify him."[17] Pionios
says that Christ was a man and, according to the Jews, died a
violent (and therefore disgraceful) death, like a criminal, but,

[15] Robert *Martyre*, pp. 54–5.
[16] *Mart. Pionii* 4.11–12, with the commentary of Robert *Martyre*.
[17] *Mart. Pionii* 13.2.

he asks, "What other 'criminal' has filled the entire world with his disciples? What other 'criminal' has had his disciples and others with them to die for the name of their master?"[18] (I shall return in the fourth chapter to the key word, βιοθανής, in this passage.) As for Jewish charges of Christian necromancy, Pionios launches into a fervid account of Saul's Biblical effort to bring up Samuel the Prophet through a woman who specialized in necromancy. Indeed, according to the Bible, the woman did succeed in bringing up Samuel to answer a few questions.[19]

Both the substance and the rhetorical argument in Pionios's speeches point to their being, in large part, drawn from the σύγγραμμα that Pionios himself composed. The language reinforces this inference. When Pionios is interrogated by the νεωκόρος at Smyrna (a certain Polemon), the question put to him after "Are you a Christian?" is "Of what church?" (ποίας ἐκκλησίας;)[20] Although Polemon may perhaps have used the word ἐκκλησία, it is not very likely. A polytheist interrogating a Christian was not likely to use the word ἐκκλησία – as opposed to a more neutral term – to distinguish one Christian sect from another. Pionios, on the other hand, would have given his transcription of the interrogation in a form that would be readily comprehensible to the Christian readership that he had in mind. The more neutral term θρησκεία appears in the record of an interrogation later in this same martyrdom when there is no question of the use of Pionios's σύγγραμμα.[21] So the earlier ἐκκλησία is not likely to reflect the redactor's vocabulary, but Pionios's own.

Apart from Christian terminology, Pionios's Greek shows signs of the living language. The most conspicuous case is the recurring use of ναί simply to mean "yes" – a word that has served the Greeks in their talk from Plato to the present. More striking are certain words that appear here with a meaning

---

[18] *Mart. Pionii* 13.4–5.　　[19] *Mart. Pionii* 14.2–14, with Robert *Martyre, ad loc.*
[20] *Mart. Pionii* 9.2.　　[21] *Mart. Pionii* 19.4

that does not reappear again until the Byzantine Greek of a later age. The most revealing diction occurs precisely in Pionios's own account of life in the prison where he was actually writing his σύγγραμμα. The bribes offered to the guards are described here as συνήθη, a usage rarely attested in literary texts and showing up next (in the form συνήθεια) in provincial inscriptions of some two centuries later.[22] The guards' taking a portion of the gifts sent to the prisoners as a kind of bribe for good treatment is expressed by the participle ἐπιφιλανθρω-πευόμενοι, a *hapax* with the prefix ἐπι-.[23] A particularly interesting case in this context, because so rare, is the use of φιλολογεῖν to describe how the prisoners passed their time. They had, we are told, leisure to indulge in φιλολογεῖν. This does not mean, as has normally been assumed, simple conversation. It means, as Louis Robert has astutely demonstrated, "to engage in dialectical argument," – a late Greek and Byzantine usage.[24]

As for the narrative supposedly left by Perpetua before her martyrdom at Carthage, it was E. R. Dodds, in his Wiles Lectures of exactly thirty years ago (*Pagan and Christian in an Age of Anxiety*), who rightly observed that a fundamental document incorporated in the extant Greek and Latin versions of her martyrdom is "a sort of prison diary kept by Perpetua while awaiting execution."[25] This diary includes an account of four dreams of remarkable character, redolent of the social world to which Perpetua belonged. Dodds sensitively and firmly distinguished the material in Perpetua's journal from the writings of a redactor, who may well be the same as the eyewitness of the climactic latter part of the narrative. We have already observed how style and rhetoric

---

[22] *Mart. Pionii* 11.5. Cf. *OGIS* 521.16 and *SEG* IX.365.16 ff. The word συνήθη has been regularly misunderstood; cf. Robert *Martyre*, pp. 76–7.

[23] *Mart. Pionii* 11.4. See Robert *Martyre*, p. 76.

[24] *Mart. Pionii* 11.7: Robert *Martyre*, p. 77.

[25] E. R. Dodds, *Pagan and Christian in an Age of Anxiety* (Cambridge, 1965), p. 48.

can distinguish the unique contribution of Pionios to the account of his own martyrdom. Similarly, Dodds observes,

> in the first place, Perpetua's simple style is very different from the rhetorical cleverness of the redactor [whom many believe, with good reason, to have been none other than Tertullian] ... And while I take it as now pretty well established that the redactor's original language was Latin, there are fairly strong reasons for thinking that the diary was originally kept in Greek. Secondly, the diary is entirely free from marvels, and the dreams it reports are entirely dream-like.[26]

In a long and important article Louis Robert was able to annotate the dreams of Perpetua, on the basis of the agonistic institutions of the age and the language that described it.[27] Dodds, from his unique perspective of psychoanalysis and his own well-known personal exploration of the occult, was able with equal authority to declare that the dreams of Perpetua could reasonably represent the dreaming of the martyr herself.

In the case of Perpetua the text of the martyrdom not only mentions Perpetua's journal, just as the text of the Pionios martyrdom mentioned the σύγγραμμα of Pionios. The redactor in this case explicitly says that the narrative is drawn from her account: "The whole account of the martyrdom written in her own hand and according to her own ideas [*suo senso* in Latin, and τῷ voῖ in Greek]."[28] Later the narration includes Perpetua's own words as she comes to the foreordained conclusion: "So much for what I did up until the eve of the public spectacle. About what is going to happen at that spectacle, let him write of it who will!"[29] The Greek at this point is far more

---

[26] Dodds, *Pagan and Christian*, pp. 49–50. For a different perspective, cf. B. D. Shaw, "The Passion of Perpetua," *Past and Present* no. 139 (1993), 3–45, especially p. 28, n. 63.

[27] L. Robert, "Une vision de Perpétue martyre à Carthage en 203," *Comptes rendus de l'Acad. des Inscr. et Belles-Lettres* (1982), 228–76.

[28] *Mart. Perpet.* 2.3. Cf. 14.1

[29] *Mart. Perpet.* 10.15: *hoc usque in pridie muneris egi; ipsius autem muneris actum, si quis voluerit, scribat.*

precise than the Latin, and in my opinion it serves as a guarantee that Perpetua did indeed write in Greek. "I have written these things up until the eve of the φιλοτιμίαι."[30] This stunning use of a word that we normally associate with ambition, benefaction, and high civic achievement is used by Perpetua to describe her own torture and execution. But the Latin equivalent for φιλοτιμία is *munus*, and rightly so. In Greek of this period φιλοτιμία denotes precisely a public spectacle offered by a civic magistrate.[31] When *munus* is again repeated in the Latin version, however, as Perpetua observes that anyone who wishes can write of what is going to happen, the Greek is markedly more vivid, "what is going to happen in the amphitheater" (τὰ ἐν τῷ ἀμφιθεάτρῳ γενησόμενα). The use of φιλοτιμία and the variant naming the amphitheater, when the Latin has *munus* both times, provide powerful support for the view that Perpetua wrote her account in Greek.

Whether Perpetua's words, in whatever language, allow us to hear an authentic and distinctive woman's voice, as two scholars have independently claimed in the last few years,[32] is much more doubtful. How would we tell? The fuller and idiomatic Greek belongs to its time but certainly not to one sex, and the Latin is even less distinctive. As for Saturus, whose vision is also recorded in the same martyrdom, there is no clear indication whether he wrote his account in Greek.[33] On the other hand, it is likely once again to be an authentic document both from the simplicity of its narration and the social context within which the action of the dream takes place.

Eyewitness narrations serve, in the most substantial of the Acts of the martyrs, to supplement the documentary evidence

[30] *Mart. Perpet.* 10.15: ταῦτα ἕως πρὸ μιᾶς τῶν φιλοτιμιῶν ἔγραψα. τὰ ἐν τῷ ἀμφιθεάτρῳ γενησόμενα ὁ θέλων συγγραψάτω.
[31] On φιλοτιμία, see the references in Robert, *Martyre*, p. 102.
[32] Pauline Schmitt-Pantel (ed.), *A History of Women in the West*, vol. 1 (Cambridge, Mass., 1992), p. 473; B. D. Shaw, "The Passion of Perpetua."
[33] But he did write it with his own hand: *Mart. Perpet.* 11.1.

from the martyrs themselves or from the Roman bureaucracy. The redactor of the martyrdom of Polycarp says explicitly that the entire story was transcribed by a certain otherwise unknown Gaius from a document of Irenaeus, with whom Polycarp had lived.[34] The redactor identifies himself as a man by the name of Socrates who worked at Corinth, and the text we possess records that a certain Pionios subsequently transcribed the whole narrative all over again after seeing Polycarp in a vision.[35] Presumably the original version of the martyrdom ended with Socrates's revelation of his identity. In any case, Irenaeus is identified as the eyewitness.

As we have observed in the martyrdom of Pionios a century later, the eyewitness seems to take over just after the martyr's own reference to the apostate who had tried to force "us." The text changes noticeably in style and substance at this point with the words, "Later the proconsul came to Smyrna. Pionios was brought before him on the twelfth of March and gave testimony with the minutes being taken down by a secretary."[36] The interrogation that follows may perhaps be taken from the official record or have been put down by the eyewitness, who subsequently recorded the actual death of the martyr. The proconsul's questioning in the interrogation is distinctive. This is the point at which, instead of asking, as in Pionios's version of an earlier protocol, "To which church do you belong?", the proconsul asks, "What is the cult or sect to which you belong?" (Ποίαν θρησκείαν ἢ αἵρεσιν ἔχεις;) Here presumably we hear the language regularly used in interrogations of this kind, altered in the earlier instance by the martyr himself. The eyewitness of the death of Pionios not only describes the martyr's immolation but introduces it with a most unusual illustration of the martyr's joy. Just after Pionios has been nailed down, the executioner says to him helpfully, "Change your mind and the nails will be taken out." Where-

---

[34] *Mart. Polycarpi* 22.2.   [35] *Mart. Polycarpi* 22.3.   [36] *Mart. Pionii* 19.1

upon Pionios replies with good-humored composure, "I feel that they are in to stay."[37]

The spectacular demise of Perpetua and others in the amphitheater at Carthage is, as Dodds observed, related in a grandiose style that suggests a highly educated author. The original language in this case appears to be Latin, and, as we have noted, many have reasonably detected in this text the Latinity of Tertullian. Whether Tertullian or not, the author knows how to compose an operatic finale. Yet the circumstantial detail leaves little doubt that this is an account of one who was there. Perpetua's protest at being asked to put on the garb of a priestess of Ceres carries real conviction, and the acquiescence of the military tribune provokes the author to an epigram worthy of the great Tertullian, if not actually by him: "Injustice acknowledged justice" (*agnovit iniustitia iustitiam*).[38] Again, at a later stage in the proceedings when the women to be martyred were stripped naked and put in nets to be taken into the arena, the horror of the crowd before this clearly inappropriate humiliation is registered by the narrator: *horruit populus*.[39]

In many ways, the third category of documentation in the written record of early martyrdoms is that of the formal protocol of interrogations conducted by Roman magistrates. The account of the martyrdom of Pionios includes two references to stenographers present at the hearings.[40] The sequence of questioning there and in several other Martyr Acts – most strikingly the Acts of Justin Martyr and the Scillitan martyrs – suggests a protocol of the Roman bureaucracy. In most cases the Roman magistrate tries his best to dissuade the Christian defendant from going to martyrdom and urges a resolution of the crisis by his simply acknowledging the divinity of the Roman emperor, swearing by his genius, sacri-

---

[37] *Mart. Pionii* 21.3–4.   [38] *Mart. Perpet.* 18.6.   [39] *Mart. Perpet.* 20.2.
[40] *Mart. Pionii* 9.1 (γράφοντος τοῦ νοταρίου πάντα); cf. 19.1 (γενομένων ὑπομνημάτων τῶν ὑποτεταγμένων).

ficing to him, and offering prayers. It is clear that the give-and-take of question and answer follows a form that is well documented in the papyri of the Roman imperial period.

The interrogations and the protocols connected with them are particularly important in marking the great differences between Christian martyrdoms and those episodes of courageous resistance that were later categorized among the Jews as *qidduš ha-shem* (sanctification of the name). The important collection of studies, assembled by J. W. van Henten under the title *The Origin of Jewish Martyrology*, emphasizes the complete lack of interrogation procedures in Jewish literature on this subject.[41] When the Jews finally acquired the idea of martyrdom in late antiquity, the Roman state had by then become a Christian enterprise. Governors no longer quizzed Christians about their willingness to sacrifice to the emperor. The Jewish martyrs resemble far more the post-Constantinian Christian martyrs than any of those of the earlier period. This constitutes another strong reason for rejecting a Jewish tradition as the source of the concept of martyr, and at the same time it shows the uniquely Roman character of the early inquisitions.

To return to the Martyr Acts, in 1966 Revel A. Coles published his important study of "Reports of Proceedings in Papyri," based largely on secular documents but including brief comparisons with the martyr literature.[42] He was able to isolate the distinctive elements of the protocols. There were normally four main parts: introductory formulae concerning the interrogation, the actual question-and-answer process, the decision on the part of the magistrate, and a concluding section. Many, if not most, of the early Martyr Acts include interrogations preceded by a record of the presiding magistrate and the interrogator, and sometimes reference to a stenographer. Thus we can assume that we have a relatively close

---

[41] van Henten, *Die Entstehung.*

[42] Revel A. Coles, *Reports of Proceedings in Papyri*, Papyrologica Bruxellensia 4 (Brussels, 1966).

transcript of what actually took place. In one instance the minutes of a hearing were actually read out. These are called by the Latin term *acta* in Greek and are mentioned in the martyrdom of Apollonius.[43] The *Acts of Cyprian* open, somewhat uncharacteristically, with a reference to a document transmitted to the proconsul from the Emperors Valerian and Gallienus.[44]

Although the minutes of the proceedings are sometimes called ἄκτα in the papyri, the more conventional term is ὑπομνηματισμοί, an expression which also finds a place in the Martyr Acts at one point, in the form ὑπομνήματα: ὑπομνήματα are said explicitly to be the basis of the account of the martyrdoms of Agape, Eirene, and Chione at Salonike.[45] There is also an interesting instance of the Latin word for a stenographer, νοτάριος, appearing in the *Martyrdom of Pionios* in Greek.[46] The word was simply taken over from Latin, *notarius*, just as it is in some of the Greek papyri.

The written record for the early martyrdoms can thus be seen in these many areas to incorporate a substantial amount of authentic material that places the martyrdoms securely in the context of the Roman empire. These texts, that responded to the needs of readers in much the same way as fiction did, are precious repositories of authentic historical material. As both martyrology and hagiography developed in the centuries after Constantine, the historical content of such narratives shrank perceptibly, although it never disappeared altogether, and the more surprising revelations of early Christianity were in some cases altered, in others eliminated. In the early Greek recension of the martyrdom of Carpus, a woman standing by the burning pile of wood was so enraptured by the spectacle of Carpus's demise that she took off

---

[43] *Mart. Apollonii* 11: ἀναγνωσθήτω τὰ ἄκτα Ἀπολλώ.   [44] *Mart. Cypr.* 1.1.
[45] *Mart. Agap. et al.* 2.3: τὰ δὲ πραχθέντα περὶ αὐτῶν ὑπομνήματά ἐστιν τὰ ὑποτεταγμένα.
[46] See n. 40 above.

her clothes and threw herself on the pyre and was consumed by the flames. But in the later Latin recension she is subjected to an interrogation by the proconsul and formally sentenced to death.[47] Such rewriting of the story clearly reflects the later Christian repudiation of voluntary martyrs.

We have already seen that the vivid and detailed accounts of Christian apostates in the σύγγραμμα of Pionios were largely excised from the text of the *Martyrdom* in the Armenian, Slavonic, and Latin translations of the Byzantine and early Renaissance periods. Similarly the parallel drawn between Christ and Socrates in the speeches of both Pionios and Apollonius, incorporated in the Martyr Acts of both these figures, reflects a generous parallelism between saintly pagans (Socrates, in particular) and saintly Christians, a parallelism that the Church subsequently repudiated.[48] It was a parallelism in which Tertullian revelled, a parallelism that made a good classical education so meaningful for an early Christian. But Augustine deplored all this, and Socrates was transformed from a proto-saint into a kind of polytheist Jesus, a hero of Julian the Apostate.

The pre-Constantinian Martyr Acts are precious remnants of a lost world. They contain authoritative documentary material, and they allow us – indeed compel us – to search for the roots of martyrdom in the second and third centuries of the Roman empire. Above all, they shed a bright light on the dark space between the Gospels and hagiography.

---

[47] *Mart. Carpi* (Greek) 44, (Latin) 6.1–4.
[48] See the first chapter above, with n. 25.

III

The civic role of martyrs

The early martyrdoms in the period down to Constantine are a conspicuously urban affair. They do not occur in the mountainous regions of Greece, or in the remote parts of central Anatolia, or in the near eastern steppe, or on the fringes of the Sahara in North Africa. For the most part, they take place in the greatest cities of the Roman world, predominantly in the eastern part of it. Apart from Justin at Rome and the group of martyrs at Lyon in France, the early martyrdoms provide a check-list of the most prosperous and important cities of the eastern Roman empire: Pergamum, Smyrna, Caesarea by the Sea, Carthage, Alexandria. In Greece, it is Thessalonica that has its martyrs, not Athens, and this is a proper reflection of the relative importance of the two places at that time. It was only in the period just before Constantine that there was a conspicuous deviation from this pattern of urban martyrdoms.[1]

The spread of Christianity into the rank and file of the Roman army (and perhaps also the increasing importance of soldier-emperors in the third century) led to the first group of

---

[1] For the locations of the various pre-Constantinian martyrdoms, see the collected *Acta* in R. Knopf, G. Krüger, T. Ruhbach, *Ausgewählte Märtyrerakten* (Tübingen, 1965), or in H. Musurillo, *Acts of the Christian Martyrs* (Oxford, 1972) – an unreliable work, which a new edition prepared by A. Birley will soon replace. For the emergence of martyrdom as a spiritual ideal in rural Egypt in the later third century, as shown in the Apocalypse of Elijah, see David Frankfurter, "The Cult of Martyrs in Egypt before Constantine," *Vigiliae Christianae* 48 (1994), 25–47.

soldier-martyrs, as reflected in the martyrdom at Durostorum on the Danube. To the Diocletianic age, on the eve of the Christian empire, martyrological literature was to assign many more soldier-martyrs, who would bring to reality the traditional metaphor of fighting in the cause of Christ. But for more than a century martyrdom had been an essentially urban manifestation of Christian zeal.

/ From the Christian point of view, martyrdom in a city provided the greatest possible visibility for the cause of the nascent Church, and it simultaneously exposed the Roman administrative machinery to the greatest possible embarrassment/ Obviously a martyrdom could not occur unless a Roman magistrate chose to impose a death penalty on a confessing Christian. This means that the apparatus of the Roman court procedure in the provinces, the so-called *cognitio* procedure, was a prerequisite for the infliction of the death penalty.[2] Although provincial governors regularly toured their provinces in order to hold assizes in the principal rural settlements and facilitate the administration of justice across the region, the martyrs regularly showed up in the big cities. It was hardly in the interest of advancing the case for Christianity to suffer martyrdom in a place where few could witness it. The involvement of large crowds or even, as in the case of Pionios, a substantial part of the whole local population, was an important part of city life. Martyrs contributed to the spectacles of blood sport in the amphitheater – confrontations with wild beasts and with gladiators, to say nothing of spectacular immolations.[3] They served to unite non-Christian citizens in the expression of prejudice, most

[2] See G. E. M. de Ste Croix, "Why Were the Early Christians Persecuted?," *Past and Present* no. 26 (1963), 6–38. especially pp. 11–13 on *cognitio extra ordinem*.

[3] D. Potter, "Martyrdom and Spectacle," in *Theater and Society in the Classical World*, ed. R. Scodel (Ann Arbor, 1993), pp. 53–88.

conspicuously in the combined hostility of Jews and poly-theists toward the Christians.[4]

The *Acts of Cyprian*, recording the martyrdom of the North African bishop in the third century, provide a good illustration of the centrality of the urban setting in the history of early martyrs. At Carthage the proconsul informed Cyprian of a document he had recently received from the Emperors Valerian and Gallienus, instructing all those who did not adhere to Roman religious beliefs at least to acknowledge Roman ceremonial rites. Cyprian of course refused to oblige, and the proconsul accordingly proposed that he be exiled to a town in the country well outside of Carthage. This was a clever and humane device, evidently designed to avoid the public drama of a trial and the sensational spectacle of an execution. In accepting the proconsul's proposal, Cyprian effectively removed himself from martyrdom at that time. But the successor to that governor was more aggressive in his determination to deal with the Christians and brought Cyprian back into Carthage. Since it had already been revealed to the bishop that he was to be martyred, he understood that this restoration to the capital city meant the first step in procedures that would end in his martyrdom. After the due process of interrogation before the new proconsul, Cyprian was condemned and subsequently beheaded.

According to the *Acts of Cyprian*, a crowd from the bishop's flock accompanied him to his death and cried out to be executed along with him.[5] Although voluntary martyrdom was something that Cyprian himself had explicitly condemned, enthusiasm for it was clearly far from spent. The presence of this crowd is reminiscent of similar scenes throughout the early Martyr Acts and serves to emphasize the

---

[4] Cf. M. Simon, *Verus Israël: étude sur les relations entre Chrétiens et Juifs dans l'Empire romain* (Paris, 1948; with supplement 1964).

[5] *Acta Cypriani* 5.1: *post eius sententiam populus fratrum dicebat: et nos cum eo decollemur.*

43

important role of the exemplary martyrs as teachers and leaders of the Christian communities in the Roman provinces. Men like Cyprian and Pionios in the third century and Polycarp in the second were the Christian equivalent of the famous teachers and sophists who enlivened and adorned the intellectual and social life of those two centuries. The sophists, who had their own enthusiastic supporters, zealous in ways not unlike that of the followers of Christ, were chronicled by the third-century writer Philostratus and have been much studied in the last thirty years.[6] The parallel between them and many of the more flamboyant leaders of the Christians in this period was well drawn by Timothy Barnes at the end of his book on Tertullian in a chapter entitled "The Christian Sophist."[7] The age of the martyrs and the age of the sophists is largely one and the same. The culture from which both groups came and upon which both depended for their power of communication was likewise the same. It was a Graeco-Roman culture in which pagans and Christians alike could share.

During the interrogation of Polycarp, after the herald proclaimed that the defendant had acknowledged that he was a Christian, the entire crowd of pagans and Jews who lived in Smyrna shouted out loud, "This is the teacher of Asia, the father of the Christians, the destroyer of our gods."[8] The words "teacher" (διδάσκαλος) and "father" (πατήρ) were precisely the words that were used of the great sophists. These terms suggest not only the broad influence of a leader such as Polycarp but the passionate devotion that was felt for him. The term "father" for a particularly respected teacher was conspicuous in the age of the great sophists. (It has sometimes even led, embarrassingly, to confusion in the construction of genealogical tables.) Interpreting a community of teacher and

---

[6] G. W. Bowersock, *Greek Sophists in the Roman Empire* (Oxford, 1969); G. Anderson, *The Second Sophistic* (London, 1993).

[7] T. D. Barnes, *Tertullian* (Oxford, 1971), pp. 211–32.   [8] *Mart. Polycarpi* 12.2.

disciples as a kind of spiritual family was characteristic of the ancient philosophical and rhetorical schools, for which subsequent generations constituted what was known as the διαδοχή or "succession."[9] The adaptation of this language by the Christian Church was a reflection of that early phase of Christianity, which Paul was the first to undermine, in which spiritual bonds took precedence over family ties.[10] Jesus's doctrine that anyone who does the will of God, "the same is my brother, and my sister, and my mother" (Mark 3.35), fit easily into the pattern of allegiances created by leading polytheist philosophers and sophists. Finally, of course, it led to the traditional use of "father," "sister," "brother," "son," and "daughter" in clerical contexts. Neither the polytheists nor the Christians, however, used more remote kinship terminology for their spiritual relationship.

Christians regarded themselves as fellow students of their master, and ultimately as all fellow students together of the ultimate master, Jesus Christ. The word συμμαθηταί, "fellow learners," is applied to the followers of Polycarp in the narrative of his martyrdom.[11] Even at the end of his life Polycarp's work as a teacher is emphasized again in a way that puts his paedagogic role on an equal level with his role as a martyr: οὐ μόνον διδάσκαλος γενόμενος ἐπίσημος ἀλλὰ καὶ μάρτυς ἔξοχος: "he was not only an outstanding teacher but also an eminent martyr."[12] The συμμαθηταί who followed him all considered themselves brothers – brothers in Christ to be sure, but brothers in that narrower community of discipleship.

Similar language is used in the account of the interrogation of the martyr Papylus at Pergamum. The proconsul asked, "Do you have any children?" and Papylus replied, "Yes, many, by God's grace" (Τέκνα ἔχεις; – καὶ πολλὰ διὰ τὸν

---

[9] Cf. V. Nutton, "Herodes and Gordian," *Latomus* 29 (1970), 725, on the alleged descent of Gordian from Herodes as opposed to a paedagogical succession.

[10] See now E. Pagels, *Adam, Eve, and the Serpent* (New York, 1988), pp. 15–20.

[11] *Mart. Polycarpi* 17.3. [12] *Mart. Polycarpi* 19.1.

θεόν). It was left to one person in the attendant crowd, evidently someone who was Christian, to provide an explanation to the governor: "He means he has children by virtue of the faith which the Christians repose in him" (κατὰ τὴν πίστιν αὐτοῦ τῶν Χριστιανῶν λέγει τέκνα ἔχειν). That interpretation led to an explosive reaction from the proconsul, who demanded to know why Papylus lied in saying that he had children. To this, in turn, Papylus declared, "May I inform you that I am not lying but telling the truth. I have children in every province and city κατὰ θεόν [in the Lord]."[13] The details of this interrogation provide a vivid commentary on the terminology found in the *Acts of Polycarp*.

An important setting for the final days of a martyr's teaching was the local prison, in which the martyr was confined pending interrogation and execution. There was usually a captive audience of other Christians as well as police officers and prison guards in the employ of the city. But others came voluntarily, including pagans who wanted to dispute with the master teacher. The scene is vividly described in the case of the incarceration of Pionios and his followers: "Nevertheless in the prison many of the pagans [πολλοὶ τῶν ἐθνῶν] came, wanting to persuade [the Christians], and yet upon hearing them they were amazed at their replies."[14]

But it was in the agora under the open sky, in the central part of the city, that a martyr could make his most powerful impact. The role of the designated martyr as teacher is superbly illustrated in the two great speeches of Pionios that are preserved in the account of his martyrdom. Since all material in this text down to the final interrogation appears to have been derived from the written record prepared in prison by Pionios himself,[15] we can have reasonable confidence that the two speeches represent essentially what Pionios said to the

---

[13] *Acta Carpi et al.* 27–32.   [14] *Mart. Pionii* 12.1.

[15] See the previous chapter on "the written record." The two speeches come in 4 and 12–14 of the *Mart. Pionii*.

crowds. Their idiomatic language and subtle arguments imply as much. With their eloquence, erudition, and complex evocation of shared culture, these speeches can easily stand comparison with the work of any great sophist of the age, Aelius Aristides, Polemo, and Herodes Atticus among the foremost. The speeches were delivered in the agora of Smyrna, and in the proximity of the temple of the two Nemesis goddesses (the Nemeseis), at which Pionios was enjoined to sacrifice to the emperor.

The martyrs' contribution to civic life and civic pride was not unlike that of the sophists in holding a mirror up to the inhabitants of the great cities. Pionios, addressing the polytheists of Smyrna, speaks to their pride in claiming Smyrna as the birthplace of Homer. He likewise speaks to their pride, well documented in inscriptions and on coins, in the beauty of the city. He invokes the text of Homer himself, whom he names as their teacher (τῷ διδασκάλῳ ὑμῶν Ὁμήρῳ), that it is not right to gloat over those who die.[16]

With similar aptness Pionios also addresses the Jews of Smyrna, who constituted an important community in that city and perhaps a particularly large part of the crowd that was listening to him. Already in the early second century, Ignatius, writing in Smyrna, commented several times on the strained relations between Jews and Christians.[17] As we saw in the previous chapter, Pionios quotes lavishly from the Old Testament, citing pertinent examples from the stories of Moses and of Solomon. He invokes Beelphagor, Sodom and Gomorrah, and the golden calf, and he makes reference to the Books of Judges, Kings, and Exodus. In a particularly brilliant exposition of truly sophistic subtlety, Pionios recounts the famous

---

[16] For these allusions, see *Mart. Pionii* 4.2–4, with the commentary by L. Robert, *Le martyre de Pionios*, ed. G. W. Bowersock and C. P. Jones (Dumbarton Oaks, 1994).

[17] Ignatius, *Epist. ad Smyrn.* 4–5, especially 4.1: προφυλάσσω δὲ ὑμᾶς ἀπὸ τῶν θηρίων τῶν ἀνθρωπομόρφων. Cf. *Epist ad Magnes.* 10.3: ἄτοπόν ἐστιν, Ἰησοῦν Χριστὸν λαλεῖν καὶ ἰουδαΐζειν.

story of the witch of Endor and the feat of necromancy by which Samuel was brought back from the dead. This story of necromancy, says Pionios, was something that he had heard discussed by Jews since he was a child.[18] This in itself is a remarkable testimony to the interaction of Jews and Christians in third-century Asia and to the significance of the Jewish population that knew Pionios. In a sense, in his two final speeches, Pionios stands as a teacher of the Jews and of the polytheists as much as a teacher of the Christians. His intellectual role in the city is not unlike that of Aelius Aristides.

The fame of the martyrs is manifest from the crowds that attended them. The Martyr Acts abound in references to the uproar of crowds. The Roman governors must have given careful thought to the time at which the formal interrogations as well as the executions would take place. There are simply too many examples of martyrdoms on major holidays to be accidental. The martyrdoms of both Polycarp and Pionios are ascribed to the Great Sabbath (the Μέγα Σάββατον), a festival still not conclusively identified but obviously one on which pagans and Jews alike were free to stay away from work.[19] They could listen to the proceedings all day and watch the spectacle unfold. The martyrdom of Perpetua was scheduled on no less an occasion than the birthday of the Emperor Geta.[20]

Sanguinary entertainments on the emperor's birthday had a long history. Well before there were any Christian martyrs, the Jews had been subjected to similar persecution in Alexandria. The Jewish philosopher Philo had protested vigorously.

---

[18] *Mart. Pionii* 14.1.   [19] See Robert, *Martyre*, p. 50.

[20] *Acta Perpet.* 7.9 (*natale tunc Getae Caesaris*) and 16.3. Cf. T. D. Barnes, "Pre-Decian *Acta Martyrum*," *Journal of Theological Studies* 19 (1968), 509–31, particularly pp. 522–3.

For rulers who administer a state upon sound principles are accustomed not to punish condemned persons until these glorious birthdays and festivals of the glorious Augusti have passed. But Flaccus on the occasion of these very festivities was committing outrage and inflicting penalty upon men who were guiltless of any crime ... I know of instances before now of persons who had been impaled when a holiday of this kind was at hand ... Flaccus ordered, not persons who had died upon crosses to be taken down, but living persons to be impaled, to whom the season offered not entire remission, but amnesty ... The spectacle was divided into acts, the first shows lasting from dawn until the third òr fourth hour were these: Jews being scourged, hanged, turned on the wheel, maltreated, led away through the midst of the orchestra the way to death, while the shows that followed this splendid exhibition were performances of dancers, mimes, flute-players, and all the other favorites of theatrical contests.[21]

The crowd could be aggressive and cruel, but it could also show compassion. The Martyr Acts reflect with apparent precision the shifting moods of the city populace and the interesting counterpoint of the martyr's interaction with it. Polycarp was no friend of the Smyrnaeans, who made a great noise (θόρυβος ἦν μέγας) when he was brought into the amphitheater.[22] He looked at them and shook his fist. Then he groaned, gazed heavenwards, and cried out, "Away with the godless ones!" The governor on the scene was therefore exceedingly cunning when he answered Polycarp's offer to give him a private lecture on Christianity. "Persuade the people," he said. To this injunction Polycarp shot back, "I consider you worthy of a speech ..., but I do not think that they deserve to have an accounting from me."[23]

By contrast Pionios won a measure of sympathy from the spectators in the agora at Smyrna. "You know," said Pionios to the crowd, "what it is to suffer famine and death and other

---

[21] Philo, *in Flacc.* 81–5 (from the translation by H. Box).
[22] *Mart. Polycarpi* 9.1.
[23] *Mart. Polycarpi* 10.2.

calamities." And someone said in reply, "You went hungry with us."[24] Pionios had shared in their famine; he was part of their city. In a similar tone the martyr Papylus declared proudly to the proconsul at Pergamum that he was a citizen (πολίτης) of the city of Thyatira.[25]

If the fame of the martyrs in life was not unlike that of the sophists, in the manner of their dying their fame was far closer to that of the great athletes and gladiators. It is not only that the dying martyrs are constantly compared in the literature to athletes, although we should not lose sight of the fact that they are.[26] In one notable case, the martyr Maturus at Lyon actually was an athlete.[27] More important is the fact that the killing of the martyrs often took the form of spectacle in the city amphitheater. Some were burned there, some were given to the beasts for bloody dismemberment, and some were nailed up to hang.

Spectacle was an important element in martyrdom in the early Church. By trying to set an example, the Roman magistrates provided an entertainment. No early martyr was taken aside discreetly and executed out of sight, just as no interrogations were conducted in small towns. In a recent important paper, David Potter has examined the phenomenon of martyrdom from the sociological perspective of spectacle, and he has brought together the many examples of public entertainment in which martyrs were the principal players.[28] But what needs to be stressed here is that the martyrdom spectacles did not import something altogether new in the urban life of those spectacles in the amphitheater that were well established and much appreciated. In other words, such spectacles fit within a pre-existing social order that shaped them, just as the role of martyr as teacher and sophist similarly fits

---

[24] *Mart. Pionii* 10.7–8.   [25] *Acta Carpi et al.* 26–7.
[26] See Robert, *Martyre*, pp. 56 and 120.
[27] *Mart. Lugdun.* 17.   [28] See Potter, "Martyrdom and Spectacle."

within a pre-existing social order that enabled philosophy and rhetoric to have so powerful an influence.

The vision of Perpetua in which she anticipates her own martyrdom in the amphitheater is, as Louis Robert has so conclusively shown, built up entirely from elements of the traditional presentation of *munera* (φιλοτιμίαι) in Carthage.[29] Perpetua sees herself in the amphitheater with a man of enormous height, whose head rises above the very top of the amphitheater itself, and whose clothes show purple garments not only falling from his two shoulders but also spread over his chest. This huge figure has shoes embroidered in gold and silver, and he carries a wand like the judge at an athletic competition or a display of gladiators.[30] The figure is thus identifiably clad in the attire of an ἀγωνοθέτης, the person who gives the spectacles (the *munera*). He wears the appropriate garb of that generous office. In Perpetua's case, she sees this oversized person as presenting her in the amphitheater for her own death in the cause of Christianity. Robert has recognized that the ἀγωνοθέτης in Perpetua's dream must be understood to be none other than Christ himself – Christ the giver of competitions, Christ the provider of spectacles that serve the will of God.[31] Tertullian had written in his address to prospective martyrs (*martyres designati*), "You are going to submit to a good ἀγών [*bonum agonem subituri estis*] in which the living God is the agonothete, the ξυστάρχης is the Holy Spirit ..., and the president of the ἀγών is Christ."[32] The language – ἀγωνοθέτης, ξυστάρχης, and president or ἐπιστάτης – is the language of the Greek ἀγῶνες. Here the relationship of God and Christ is distributed among these three parts.

---

[29] L. Robert, "Une vision de Perpétue martyre à Carthage en 203," *Comptes rendus de l'Acad. des Inscr. et Belles-Lettres* (1982), 228–76.

[30] *Mart. Perpet.* 10.8.   [31] Robert, "Une vision," pp. 257–66.

[32] Tertull., *ad mart.* 3: *bonum agonem subituri estis in quo agonothetes Deus vivus est, xystarches Spiritus sanctus ... itaque epistates vester Christus Iesus.* See Robert, "Une vision," p. 265.

All this means that the role of the martyrs in dying is conceived as a kind of public entertainment offered by God to the communities where it takes place as some kind of far more edifying transmutation of the traditional games. It also means that the early martyrs see God or Christ himself as the agent of their martyrdom, rather than the various governors that decree their deaths. This is, in other words, a performance orchestrated by God. It must have been a comforting thought. The Roman magistrates have been assigned their roles so that the performance could take place, and so that by this means the martyrs could bear their witness.

The whole drama unfolded in the conspicuous places of a city. The martyr was moved from prison to tribunal, usually in the agora and close by the temple at which sacrifice to the emperor would be enjoined. The final scene was normally set in the amphitheater, and any exception strikingly confirms the rule. The legate (and *praeses*, or governor) of Numidia had removed Marianus and Jacobus from Cirta to the military camp at Lambaesis, described ironically in the surviving *acta* as the only hostelry provided by the pagans for the just (*sola apud gentiles hospitia iustorum*).[33] The martyrs were led back for their glorious end, not, to be sure, in an amphitheater but in the river valley that surrounded the plateau of Cirta on the north and northeast.[34] Yet the deep valley itself with its high banks served as an appropriate setting (*spectaculo erat excelsa utrimque aggeris altitudo*). In the presence of the river the martyrdom could become literally, as it often was metaphorically, a second baptism.[35] The martyrs were arranged in rows and executed, theatrically and, to judge by the *acta*, in public view.

We have observed earlier that the first Martyr Acts sometimes even allow us to glimpse the tensions and backsliding of

---

[33] *Acta Mar. et Iacob.* 9.5.   [34] *Acta Mar. et Iacob.* 9–10.

[35] *Ibid.*: *nec deerat utriusque sacramenti genus, cum et baptizarentur suo sanguine et lavarentur in flumine.*

weaker Christian brethren among all the ceremonial magnificence and public pressure of the citizenry. Although redactors and copyists must have excised many details of this kind, the Greek version (and only the Greek version) of the martyrdom of Pionios documents the high emotion and human frailty that accompanied the interrogation of martyrs at Smyrna.

A certain Euctemon, who was a leader of the Christian community in the city, finally yielded to the authorities and sacrificed at the altar of the Nemeseis goddesses beside the agora. Pionios was thrust in front of him just as he was standing worshipfully at the altar. According to the narrative, which was probably (as we have argued) composed by Pionios himself, Euctemon had brought a small lamb to the temple, had it roasted, and then intended to take most of it back home once a piece had been offered in sacrifice. "He had become ridiculous," says the narrative, "because of his false oath and swearing by the emperor's fortune and the Nemeseis goddesses."[36] This is the real world of martyrs in the second century.

The most sordid contribution of the martyrs to the civic life of eastern Roman cities was undoubtedly the enforced prostitution of females. As Sabina, the consort of Pionios, was told at Smyrna when she surprised her interrogators by laughing in the eternal joy of Christ, "women who do not sacrifice are put into a brothel."[37] This was the fate of Irene, whom the prefect at Thessalonica sentenced to be exposed naked in the local whorehouse.[38] But we are told that no man dared to approach her or even to revile her. We may recall that the shock of the spectators at Carthage upon seeing the naked bodies of some of Perpetua's fellow-martyrs led the authorities to clothe those young women.[39] Similarly the meager evidence for

---

[36] *Mart. Pionii* 18.14. [37] *Mart. Pionii* 7.6. Cf. Robert, *Martyre*, pp. 68–9.
[38] *Acta Agap. et al.* 5.8.
[39] *Acta Perpet.* 20.2–3.

punishment by prostitution suggests that the civic interest in such exploitation of female martyrs may have been less than Roman officials anticipated. Revulsion on the part of spectators and clients may have even worked to the Christians' advantage in promoting their cause. So the civic setting could obviously be more than simple stage for the enactment of martyrdom.

Martyrdom was thus solidly anchored in the civic life of the Graeco-Roman world of the Roman empire. It ran its course in the great urban spaces of the agora and the amphitheater, the principal settings for public discourse and for public spectacle. It depended upon the urban rituals of the imperial cult and the interrogation protocols of local and provincial magistrates. The prisons and brothels of the cities gave further opportunities for the display of a martyr's faith.

/ The urban character of martyrdom meant that Christians who chose not to be martyred in a persecution had the option of leaving their city./ They could invoke Matthew 10.23, "When they persecute you in this city, flee ye into another." Tertullian wrestled throughout his career with the implications of this command and addressed them at length in his *De Fuga in persecutione*. He condemned flight, as we should expect of a man with a Montanist background. Clement of Alexandria, on the other hand, did not, and indeed he acted on his principle. The debate over flight is striking in its fundamental assumption that escape – as opposed to apostasy – might be a possible alternative for a Christian. And that escape would invariably be from a city.

Christians understandably drew their inspiration from the death of Jesus Christ himself as well as from some early internecine struggles with heretical Christians and conflicts with the traditional Jews of Palestine. But from the point at which martyrdom emerges in the historical record as a recognizable Christian institution, it has both its sophistic and agonistic components, solidly placed in Graeco-Roman urban space. It may be suggested that without these components martyrdom as Christians understood it in the history of their early Church simply could not have existed. Martyrdom served as a catalyst of the intellectual and social rituals of the city by holding a mirror to the traditional functions of the agora and the amphitheater as well as to the urban environment to which they belonged – prison, temple, and brothel. Furthermore, crowds were an essential part of the martyrdoms, and these could only be mustered in sufficient numbers in the big cities.

Later, when the first soldier-martyrs appear, the military context provided an appropriate analogue to the civic one. Once again, what took place was anchored in a social and ceremonial context that involved a reworking of the traditional institutional forms. These were the *cognitio* procedure of trial and the condemnation to death as an athlete of God. The army provided the necessary community (in place of an urban citizenry), and the army's discipline the necessary ritual organization (in place of a city's cults). Early martyrdom absolutely presupposed self-sacrifice within some kind of a community.

In addition, although there would have been no martyrdom without persecution, the dream of Perpetua in which God himself appears as an actual producer or manager of the games in which the martyrs died symbolizes a belief evidently held by many, perhaps even most Christians, namely that the ultimate initiative for what happened in these bloody celebrations came from God himself. And, if this is not consonant with the theology of martyrdom as expounded by Clement in the fourth book of his *Stromateis*, an important text to which we shall return in the next chapter, it is entirely consistent with the view of Tertullian in his celebrated address known as the *Scorpiace*, where he declares explicitly that God contrived to make martyrdom possible precisely by his prohibition of idolatry. If he had not forbidden Christians to commit idolatry, there would have been no martyrdoms at all (*aliter enim martyria non evenerint*). It was Tertullian's understanding that God fully intended the executions to provide the sanguinary witness of His martyrs. God's will made a *locus martyriis*, as Tertullian explained it, from the injunctions against idolatry (*ex praeceptis prohibitae semper . . . idololatriae*).[40]

The problem here is that God's will could actually have been subverted, had the Romans chosen to allow the Christians not to practice idolatry, just as, indeed, they allowed the Jews. But it was precisely the Christians' vigorous participation in the civic life and intellectual traditions of the Graeco-Roman world that grounded their martyrdoms in the life of their great cities. The Jews, by contrast, had conspicuously chosen a different path by remaining altogether separate in their conduct of life, except, of course, on those public occasions when the Christian martyrs united them with the polytheists in giving expression to a common hostility. But we find no Jewish rabbis teaching the people of Smyrna or Pergamum or Carthage, as Polycarp, Papylus, and Cyprian did.

It may be said that the form of the early martyrdoms was conditioned and nurtured by the traditional pagan institutions of Graeco-Roman urban life, and that it was inconceivable without it. That, it may be suggested, is why Christian martyrdom as we know it arose first in Asia Minor and not in the part of Palestine where Christianity was born. Early Christian sacrifice through martyrdom was very different from the sacrifice and bloodless witnessing (or confession) of late antiquity: anchorites in the desert, pillar saints in their aerial isolation, holy men in remote and less remote places, ascetics of all kinds. These were displays of piety that were better suited to a Christian empire. The first martyrs, by contrast, achieved their renown in a polytheist world. Their witnessing

[40] Tertull., *Scorp.* 4.

presupposed that they espoused a *religio illicita* that was subject to the peculiar dynamics of persecution. Thus the Lives of the Saints differed inevitably from the Acts of the Martyrs. The urban stage was no longer necessary.

IV

Martyrdom and suicide

Among the most memorable scenes in the history of Roman persecution of the early Church is that crowd of zealous Christians pleading with Arrius Antoninus, a proconsul of Asia in the second century, to put them to death as martyrs.[1] His bemused and anguished response directed these eager souls to the nearest available ropes and cliffs. Similar enthusiasm for martyrdom was no less apparent among some who, when condemned to die, betrayed impatience in waiting for their ultimate dissolution. In the narrative of the *Martyrdom of Polycarp*, we hear of the most noble Germanicus, who, when condemned to fight with wild beasts, rebuked the emperor who tried to dissuade him from self-destruction by dragging an animal directly on top of himself.[2] In this way, says the writer, the noble Germanicus chose to be liberated all the more quickly from an unjust and lawless life. In an early version of the *Martyrdom of Agathonike*, the martyr takes off her clothes and throws herself voluntarily upon the pyre.[3]

Such enthusiasm for martyrdom is mirrored in the frequent reports of radiant joy, smiles, and even laughter among the Christians on their way to a martyr's death. During the interrogation of Pionios, his companion Sabina smiled when Pionios said that it was far worse to burn after death than to be burned alive. The νεωκόρος (temple warden) was astonished by his reaction and asked incredulously, "You are laughing?"

---

[1] See the beginning of chapter i above.   [2] *Mart. Polycarpi* 3.1.
[3] *Mart. Carpi et al.* 44 (Agathonike).

Whereupon she replied confidently, "If God so wills, yes. We are Christians, and those who believe in Christ will laugh unhesitatingly in everlasting joy."[4] Pionios himself, who was normally of a conspicuously pale complexion, turned positively ruddy with joy as he approached his own martyrdom.[5] When Pamphylus was nailed to a stake, he was seen to look happy and smiling, and in response to a question he answered, "I saw the glory of my God, and I rejoiced that I was free."[6] The Carthaginian martyr Perpetua declared, in her account of her condemnation, that, when she and her companions were sentenced to death, they returned to the prison in high spirits: in the Latin text, *hilares descendimus ad carcerem*.[7] Her good cheer continued as she went to her death: "Perpetua went with a shining countenance and calm step."[8]

Eagerness for martyrdom – what is described in the *Acts of the Martyrs of Lyon* as τῆς μαρτυρίας ἐπιθυμία[9] – not only maintained the martyrs in good spirits. It could make them laugh, to the great discomfort of governors. The martyrs could even be moved to make jokes. Prudentius, in his lyric verses on the crowns of martyrdom, tells the famous story of Lawrence, who addressed his judge from the grill on which he was being roasted: "This part of my body has been burned long enough," he announced. "Turn it round, and try what your hot god of fire has done." When the prefect then has the martyr turned over, he is reported to have said, "It is done [*coctum est*]. Eat it up and try whether it is better raw or roasted."[10] Prudentius acknowledges that these words were spoken in jest (*ludibundus*). But after they were uttered Lawrence looked up to heaven and reverently prayed.

The desire for death on the part of martyrs and would-be

---

[4] *Mart. Pionii* 7.5.
[5] *Mart. Pionii* 10.2: πῶς ἀεὶ χλωρὸς ὢν νῦν πυρρὸν ἔχει τὸ πρόσωπον.
[6] *Mart. Carpi et al.* 4.3.   [7] *Mart. Perpet.* 6.6.   [8] *Mart. Perpet.* 18.1–2.
[9] *Mart. Lugdun.* 29.
[10] Prudent., *Peristeph.* II.401–8.

martyrs was attentively observed by the pagans and must have been a constant source of wonder to them. Even the Christians at Rome might have been surprised in the time of Trajan to receive Ignatius's impassioned plea to them not to block his death among the wild animals.[11] (He obviously thought that his co-religionists could – and would – have interceded on his behalf.) The second-century satirist Lucian well reflects the situation in his account of the Christian phase of the flamboyant charlatan Peregrinus. Lucian tells us that as a Christian Peregrinus felt a great longing to die; and, in what is almost a parody of a scene from a Martyr Act, the satirist describes the imprisonment of Peregrinus, the visitations to the would-be martyr from the faithful, and the eagerness with which many volunteered to go to their death along with him.[12] On the other hand, the governor of Syria, who was presiding over this case, realized that the most effective penalty he could impose on such a person was simply to release him. And so, cannily, he set Peregrinus free precisely because he wanted to die.[13] This is Lucian's pungent and possibly historical version of the old joke that has the masochist say to the sadist, "Hit me," and the sadist replying, "No."

All these scenes suggest that for many, if not most, martyrs and would-be martyrs, their enthusiasm for death comes very close to a desire to commit suicide – a suicide to be arranged by an external agent but with the clear complicity of the victim. The last moments of Perpetua in the amphitheater at Carthage, as described by the Latin narrator, illustrate this well: "She took the trembling hand of the gladiator and guided it to her throat. Perhaps so great a woman could not have been killed ... if she herself had not wanted it."[14] Per-

---

[11] Ignatius, *Epist. ad Rom.* 4.1: παρακαλῶ ὑμᾶς, μὴ εὔνοια ἄκαιρος γένησθέ μοι. ἄφετέ με θηρίων εἶναι βοράν ...

[12] Lucian, *Peregr.* 12–13. The great charlatan was even hailed as a "new Socrates."

[13] Lucian, *Peregr.* 14.

[14] *Mart. Perpet.* 21.9–10, concluding: *fortasse tanta femina non aliter non potuisset occidi, quae ab immundo spiritu timebatur, nisi ipsa voluisset.*

petua, although not strictly a voluntary martyr, is being cast in that role.

This aspect of martyrdom caused considerable discussion among Christian theologians in the pre-Augustinian period, and we have already seen that Cyprian and others publicly and repeatedly condemned voluntary martyrdom. "Let no one give himself up to the pagans on his own initiative," said Cyprian.[15] But even he went to his own death with conspicuous enthusiasm and a sense of the dramatic potential of what was coming. He refused to confess and be condemned in Utica because he belonged in his own episcopal city of Carthage, and his death could be more efficacious there:

> The honor belonging to our illustrious church will be vitiated if it is in Utica that I should receive sentence upon making my confession (whereas I have been appointed as bishop over another church), and if it is from Utica that I should go forth as a martyred lord. For it is in your midst that I ought to be making my confession, it is there I ought to suffer.[16]

In his recent book entitled *From Autothanasia to Suicide: Self-Killing in Classical Antiquity*,[17] Anton van Hooff devotes a brief final section to martyrs, but greater attention might well have been accorded to the representation and evaluation of martyrdom in the general context of "self-killing." Van Hooff accepts Durckheim's famous definition of suicide as "any case of death which results, directly or indirectly, from an act, positive or negative, accomplished by the victim himself and in the knowledge that it would necessarily produce this result."[18] This definition necessarily comprehends martyrdom as well as suicide. The confusion of these categories provoked

[15] Cyprian, *Epist.* 81.1,4.
[16] Cyprian, *Epist.* 81.1.2 (translation by G. W. Clarke in his edition of the *Letters*, vol. 4 [New York, 1989], pp. 105–6).
[17] A. van Hooff, *From Autothanasia to Suicide: Self-Killing in Classical Antiquity* (London, 1990).
[18] van Hooff, *Autothanasia*, p. 6, quoting E. Durckheim, *Le suicide*, 3rd edn (Paris, 1930), p. 5.

such vehement debate among the early Christians who saw mounting enthusiasm for voluntary martyrdom that Augustine and other theologians ultimately moved to denounce suicide as incompatible with martyrdom.

The relation of these two forms of killing is made explicit and unavoidable in the works of Tertullian. If he is in fact the author of the Latin narrative on Perpetua's death the interpretation of it there would fit perfectly within the larger frame of Tertullian's thought. Both in his address to martyrs-designate and in his own *Apology*, he invokes as important parallels the noble suicides of the great pagans of the past. His examples include Heraclitus, Empedocles, Lucretia, Mucius Scaevola, Dido, Cleopatra, and even Peregrinus (who, long after he had given up Christianity, immolated himself at Olympia).[19] Tertullian's argument is a simple one: If these courageous people destroyed themselves for a false way of life, should Christians not do the same for the true way? "We want to suffer," says Tertullian, "just as a soldier wants to fight."[20] It is the profession of a Christian to suffer. It is the work of a Christian to be taken to court. By being conquered or subdued in the Roman persecutions, in Tertullian's view, the Christians are victorious. The paradox is that in defeat lies victory. This is a paradox not unlike Tertullian's view that peace can only be found in prison among the martyrs.

In other words, peace comes in struggling and in dying for a better cause than the pagans had. Suicide is understood as an honorable course in defense of one's own ideals. Tertullian's words, embedded in his sinewy Latin prose, constitute a magnificent reprise of both the language and the thought of Cicero in the *Tusculan Disputations* and of Seneca in his letters on the virtues of bearing pain in defense of one's principles. In suffering lay the anticipation of a greater good to come.

Tertullian's position is that of an old Roman pagan. His

---

[19] Tertull., *ad mart.* 4.   [20] Tertull., *Apol.* 50.

position converted Lucretia into a model for Christians in his *Exhortation to Chastity*.[21] It is the position of Cato the Younger, who took his own life upon the defeat of the republic. It is the position of Seneca, committing suicide in his bath when he realized that he would be unable to control the excesses of Nero. It is the position of other courageous philosophers of the Neronian and Flavian periods, who drew their strength from Stoic doctrines, just as Seneca had. Antisthenes, Diogenes, and other Cynics had preached a similar indifference to pain and acceptance of suicide in the cause of truth and integrity.[22] There is something distinctively Roman in Tertullian's attitude to martyrdom. If this attitude derives, as it probably does, from the so-called Montanist period of Tertullian's thought, the confluence of Roman values in an East Greek context becomes visible once again.[23] For Montanism itself was a product of Phrygia in Asia Minor.

However much some leaders of the Church attempted to dissuade volunteers for death in the Christian cause, the example of Arrius Antoninus's tribunal and the many references in the Martyr Acts to eager postulants for martyrdom show that the message simply did not get through. With orators like Tertullian, it is hardly surprising that the suicidal aspect of martyrdom remained at the forefront. Intellectuals schooled in the Latin classics would naturally have adopted a view of martyrdom that presupposed the admiration of noble suicides implicit in the tales of Lucretia, Scaevola, Dido, and others.

But the polytheist world as a whole was by no means united in its admiration of such noble suicides. An old and strong

---

[21] Tertull., *de exhort. cast.* 13.

[22] For Stoics and Cynics on suicide, see van Hooff, *Autothanasia*, pp. 188–92. Also R. Hirzel, "Der Selbstmord," *Archiv für Religionswissenschaft* 11 (1908), 417–76. For suicide as a tradition at Rome, see Y. Grisé, *Le suicide dans la Rome antique* (Montreal/Paris, 1983). For Seneca in particular, M. T. Griffin, *Seneca: A Philosopher in Politics* (Oxford, 1976), pp. 367–88 ("Mors diu meditata").

[23] Cf. T. D. Barnes, *Tertullian* (Oxford, 1971), p. 218.

prejudice, which had deep roots in Platonic philosophy, ran directly counter to the tradition so eloquently represented by Seneca and Tertullian. Plutarch, a contemporary of Ignatius of Antioch, memorably reflects the sensibilities of his fellow-Greeks in the early second century in his treatise on the virtues of women. There he tells of the mysterious affliction of the women of Miletus, who were given to hanging themselves for no evident reason. It was thought that polluted air had deranged their minds. Finally a law was proposed that all women who hanged themselves should be carried naked through the agora of the city on the way to burial. This immediately produced the desired result of stopping the suicides, and Plutarch could commend the women for staying alive in order to safeguard their modesty.[24]

Plato had been unambiguously opposed to self-destruction, and the Platonists of the Roman period, the so-called Middle Platonists, not only adopted this position but maintained it against Stoics and other political dissidents.[25] Neoplatonism, as represented by Plotinus and his successors, was emphatically opposed to any form of violence to oneself. Plotinus himself addressed the issue in a work on rational suicide, now lost, which presumably responded to the Stoic contention that one could decide reasonably to do away with oneself.[26]

Not surprisingly those Christian writers that were most conspicuously inspired by Plato – in particular Clement of Alexandria and Origen – took the same strong position against suicide.[27] Accordingly, when Augustine later formulated what was to become the standard Christian abhorrence of suicide, he had behind him both Platonic Christianity and

---

[24] Plut., *de mul. virtut.* 11, with the analysis of P. A. Stadter, *Plutarch's Historical Methods* (Cambridge, Mass., 1965), pp. 76–7.

[25] Cf. J. M. Dillon, *The Middle Platonists* (London, 1977), p. 198: "We hear of no 'Platonic Opposition' to the Principate to match the Stoic Opposition."

[26] Cf. Plotinus, *Enn.* 1.9, with van Hooff, *Autothanasia*, pp. 192–3.

[27] See Dietmar Wyrwa, *Die christliche Platonaneignung in den Stromateis des Clemens von Alexandrien* (Berlin, 1983).

polytheist Neoplatonism of the preceding centuries. But during those pre-Augustinian centuries the situation was by no means so clear as Augustine wanted it to be, and as it subsequently became. In the early third century, the time of both Tertullian and Clement, the issue of suicide was, as we have seen, central to the practice and the acceptance of martyrdom.[28] Tertullian represented, in sonorous and traditional Latinity, the old Roman point of view. Clement, by contrast, had absorbed the philosophy of Plato and addressed the subject, in his reflective and sometimes dense Greek prose, much more profoundly and less rhetorically than his eloquent contemporary.

In the fourth book of the miscellaneous writings that we know as *Stromateis*, Clement addressed the problem of martyrdom in detail. His thinking on this matter is so central to the perception of martyrs as suicides that it deserves our careful attention. Through Clement we can track the most important divisions of opinion in the early Christian Church before Augustine concerning a phenomenon that must be reckoned the single most visible manifestation of Christianity in the pagan Roman world. It was probably through martyrdom that many pagans became aware of Christianity in the first place during the second and third centuries. We have only to think of Lucian and his Peregrinus or of Antoninus the proconsul. The life and death of a Christian martyr was, as we have already discovered, something the pagans could readily comprehend through the quasi-sophistic role of a martyr when living and his part in agonistic festivals when dying.

Besides, the Graeco-Roman world had always taken a lively interest in freakish behavior. A brahman from India who burned himself up in Athens in the time of Augustus attracted considerable notice,[29] and Peregrinus, removing himself in

---

[28] Wyrwa, *Platonaneignung*, ch. 6, pp. 225–60: "Seelsorge angesichts des Martyriums."

[29] Cass. Dio 54.9.10 (Zarmarus – πυρὶ ἑαυτὸν ζῶντα ἐξέδωκεν).

exactly the same way in the second century, attracted no less.
Such events were as interesting in the Roman empire as
dwarfs, humans with only one arm, hermaphrodites, and
giraffes – all of which are known to have excited great interest.
Connoisseurs of the period will not forget that one of the most
popular sophists, Favorinus of Arles, had undescended testi-
cles – a condition that caused a feminine appearance and a
high-pitched voice that evidently only added to his personal
magnetism.[30]

Clement's analysis of martyrdom returned prudently to the
original sense of the word: "'Martyrdom' or μαρτυρία,
'bearing witness [μαρτυρία],' is a confession of faith in God,
and every soul that is purely constituted in recognition of
God, obeying His orders, is a martyr [μάρτυς], both in deed
and in word."[31] The point is important for Clement because
he wants to establish that martyrdom in the true sense does
not necessarily involve death at all. It is rather an expression
of one's commitment to the Christian God. The parallel he
draws between μαρτυρία and ὁμολογία ("confession") provides the foundation for an important distinction that was
later to be elaborated in the Church as it continued to wrestle
with the problem of sanguinary martyrdom. ὁμολογία in the
Byzantine period was to be a form of bloodless martyrdom to
which the pious could aspire without bringing on their own
self-destruction.[32]

Having established the relation between confession and
martyrdom, Clement then opens up the debate by presenting
discordant arguments heard among Christians of his time.

> Some of the heretics who misapprehend the Lord are both
> impious and cowardly in their desire to stay alive, and that is why
> they call the only true martyrdom the recognition of the true God.

[30] See L. Holford-Strevens, *Aulus Gellius* (London, 1988), pp. 72–3, on the evidence of Polemo's *Physiognomonica*.
[31] Clement, *Strom.* IV.4; 15.3.
[32] Cf. H. Delehaye, "Martyr et confesseur," *Analecta Bollandiana* 39 (1921), 20–49.

Now this is a point in which we likewise agree. But these heretics maintain that one who makes his confession through death is a murderer of himself and a suicide. And they bring forward into the discussion other clever devices for covering up their own cowardice.[33]

Clement here explicitly acknowledges that the problem of suicide had indeed been raised by certain Christian sects in their discussions of martyrdom. He is happy to acknowledge that the recognition of the true God does constitute a form of martyrdom. In fact, he had just said as much in the previous chapter that we have already cited. But here he ascribes the argument against suicide as one of many clever arguments (σοφίσματα) to cover up cowardice, to conceal the fact that these people are not actually prepared to die for their faith. Courage and cowardice are matters that Clement judges important in this debate, but he says here that he will deal with them later. He wants to affirm that his position is fundamentally different from that of the cowardly heretics, as he calls them. This is a necessary point for Clement to make before going on to say that he too is opposed to self-destruction and the encompassing of one's own death: "For we too condemn those who have leapt into death [τοὺς ἐπιπηδήσαντας τῷ θανάτῳ]. People who throw themselves in harm's way are not really Christians," says Clement, "although they share the Christian name."[34] This is strong language, and it is only the beginning.

"We say that these people are committing suicide without gaining martyrdom," says Clement, and here he uses a familiar periphrasis for suicide in later Greek: "to lead oneself out [ἐξάγειν ἑαυτόν]." This is an expression which seems to have been coined by Antisthenes, founder of Cynic philosophy, but it eventually passed into common use and became a standard designation of suicide from the Hellenistic period onward.[35]

[33] Clement, *Strom.* IV.4; 16.3.   [34] *Ibid.*
[35] See van Hooff, *Autothanasia*, pp. 140–1, 188.

And that is exactly what those Christians who provoke their own death are doing, according to Clement. They do it ἀμαρτύρως – "without securing martyrdom" or "without bearing witness." The condemnation is intensified when Clement adds, "This is the case even if these people are publicly condemned [κἂν δημοσίᾳ κολάζωνται]." In other words, securing a condemnation from a Roman magistrate is not a palliative for this kind of enthusiastic self-destruction. "They give themselves over to an empty death [θανάτῳ κενῷ], just as the gymnosophists of the Indians gave themselves in vain to the fire."[36] The allusion here to the Roman world's knowledge of self-immolation among the Indians directly connects the episodes of the brahman at Athens and Peregrinus at Olympia with the scenes of martyrdom. In addition the phrase "empty death" implicitly compares this ineffectual act with the κενοδοξία – the empty or false opinion – of pretentious teachers and sophists.[37]

Clement is obviously not only trying to detach martyrdom from suicide, with which he has plainly acknowledged it was connected in his own day. He is trying to turn the very word back into its original sense of "bearing witness." As Clement was writing in Greek he could make his argument turn on the very words μάρτυς and μαρτυρία themselves. This would not have been possible in Latin, the official language of the Roman government. Only a century or so after Clement (in all probability), the author of the Latin Acts of Marianus and Jacobus had to employ two quite different words to convey the senses of martyr and witness: *beati martyres plures Dei testes, dum ipsi ad martyrium parantur, adquirunt* ("While they were themselves readied for martyrdom, the blessed martyrs [*martyres*] recruited more witnesses [*testes*] of God").[38]

---

36 Clement, *Strom.* IV.4; 16.3.
37 See the discussion of κενοδοξία in L. Robert, *Le martyre de Pionios*, ed. G. W. Bowersock and C. P. Jones (Dumbarton Oaks, 1994), pp. 97–8.
38 *Mort. Marian. et Jacob.* 9.4. Cf. also 3.5 (*Dei testibus / martyrio glorioso*).

Clement's insistence on martyrdom as bearing witness meant granting that a distinctly non-voluntary and imposed death at the hand of a Roman magistrate would constitute only one way of achieving martyrdom, and perhaps not even the most important way. Bearing witness could be achieved by confessing the faith in a far less sanguinary manner. Clement, like Origen, who was equally steeped in Platonic philosophy, defended the original sense of martyrdom by invoking the Gospel of Luke, chapter 12, where Clement claims that Christ himself defined martyrdom.[39] Yet the word "martyr" is not actually used in that passage at all, even though Clement believes that it is περὶ τοῦ μαρτυρίου, "about martyrdom." Christ says in verse 8, "Whoever shall confess me before men, him shall the son of man also confess before the angels of God." The central word here is ὁμολογήσει. "Confession" or ὁμολογία thus becomes once again the business of bearing witness. Having reiterated this important point, Clement goes on to observe that some Christians who have not confessed by their life nonetheless do so in the courts by their voice and under torment up to the point of death (κατὰ φωνὴν ... ἐν δικαστηρίοις καὶ μέχρι θανάτου βασανιζομένους).[40] This is a subset of the confessors.

"It will be given to some," says Clement, "to make an ἀπολογία in order to strengthen others, in order that everyone may be helped both through martyrdom and through confession."[41] Clearly, Clement is not defining two separate means of help, but rather two aspects of the same thing, confession and bearing witness. ὁμολογία is the element that distinguishes those who are tormented or go to their death in making their confession and bearing their witness. The ἀπολογία is Clement's distinctive contribution to this discussion. "It is necessary for everyone," he says, "to confess, for this lies in our own hands, but it is not necessary for everyone to make

---

[39] Clement, *Strom.* IV.9; 70.1.   [40] Clement, *Strom.* IV.9; 73.1.   [41] *Ibid.*

an ἀπολογία [ἀπολογεῖσθαι], for this is not a matter that lies in our own hands." Clement could hardly be clearer in stating that violent martyrdom should under no circumstances represent an initiative on the part of the martyr. He is particularly eloquent in emphasizing the ἀπολογία rather than the violent death itself. The ἀπολογία is the inspiring statement, the eloquent confession of faith that moves others and glorifies God. That is where Clement places his emphasis. In the following chapter he strengthens his point by saying that those who offer themselves to persecuting magistrates incur the guilt of making the persecutors themselves sin by imposing their penalty. Thus the voluntary martyr becomes an accomplice in sin and a collaborator with the persecutor. Provocation produces guilt, and the would-be martyr who incites the persecution and calls for wild beasts is a completely guilty person (τέλειον αἴτιος).[42]

These are harsh words, and the fact that Clement found it necessary to devote so much time to a discussion of this issue in the early third century is in itself telling. He leaves no doubt that he has recognized among some Christians an enthusiasm for suicide that was directly inspired by the possibility of martyrdom in its bloody sense. In advocating a restoration of the original sense of "bearing witness," Clement is clearly rejecting the Roman glorification of suicide that Tertullian represents. He is rejecting the value of violent death, except when imposed on a Christian who had not sought it. In both these matters he is reflecting an essentially Greek point of view as opposed to a Roman one.

The Greek word, βιοθανής, for a person who suffered a violent death (often a criminal) carried, in the imperial period, a meaning virtually equivalent to suicide.[43] As Pionios recognized, one of the accusations levelled against the Christians was that their own founder, Jesus Christ himself, had suffered

---

[42] Clement, *Strom.* IV.10; 76–7.
[43] See the analysis by Robert in *Martyre*, pp. 84–5.

a violent death, and was therefore characterized as βιοθανής in the literal sense of the word (dying by violence, βιαιο-θάνατος, as the longer form shows clearly). But the martyr countered this argument by observing that the Jews failed to recognize that a βιοθανής is in fact one "who leads himself out of life by his own choice," in other words a suicide (expressed by the standard periphrasis).[44] Pionios invokes the current rather than the etymological meaning. So Christ must not be judged a βιοθανής in what was by then its customary sense, a sense confirmed by numerous other late Greek texts as well.

Among the Jews, as opposed to the polytheists, a person who died a violent death was understood to be in hell and could be used for nefarious magical purposes in working evil on other people.[45] An aura of the unnatural, the inhuman, and the diabolical attached to the victim of violent death. This point of view was, of course, utterly inconsistent with martyr-dom as it subsequently developed, with its many violent deaths and quasi-suicides, but it remained perfectly consistent with martyrdom in its original sense of bearing witness. Pionios implicitly and Clement explicitly dissociated suicide from Christian sacrifice, and their opinion was therefore wholly compatible with the views of polytheists and Jews alike. The transformation of Greek βιοθανής into a word for a suicide not only reflected a deep-seated Greek abhorrence of self-destruction: it reflected an era that saw, for the first time, a proliferation of apparent suicides by violent death. The re-definition of βιοθανής occurred within the same chrono-logical frame as the redefinition of μάρτυς. And it may be suggested that this was no accident.

Without the glorification of suicide in the Roman tradition, the development of martyrdom in the second and third cen-turies would have been unthinkable. The hordes of voluntary

---

[44] *Mart. Pionii* 13.3–7.
[45] For Jews and necromancy, see the references in Robert, *Martyre*, pp. 85–6.

martyrs would never have existed. Both Greek and Jewish traditions stood against them. Without Rome, a μάρτυς would have remained what he had always been, a "witness" and no more. But the spread of the Roman *imperium* brought with it the glorification of Lucretia and Scaevola in legend and the heroic suicides of Stoic philosophers in recent memory. Tertullian, the greatest Christian disciple of Rome's culture and language, found himself naturally cast in the role of apologist for all those who sought martyrdom. His African compatriot of the next generation, Cyprian, was less of a rhetorician and more of a thinker. The awkward Latin in which he tried to deplore the ambitions of voluntary martyrs perhaps reflects the hard problem of rooting out of Roman culture an element that was so uncongenial to the Jewish and Greek worlds in which Christianity arose.

It was not until Augustine that the Church had a clear, forceful, and definitive injunction against suicide. The seriousness and detail of Augustine's treatment of the issue in the first book of the *City of God* shows that the debate about suicide was still lively, especially in the Latin West. The heretical Donatists continued to display the spirit of Tertullian. Writing in Latin, Augustine took as his prime example the case of Lucretia, presumably because it was still as compelling to many brought up in the Latin rhetorical schools as it had been to Tertullian two centuries before. Doubtless in response to such a readership Augustine actually includes an excerpt from a Latin declamation on Lucretia in the first of his chapters on her suicide. He cites with approval the paradox *duo fuerunt et adulterium unus admisit* ("There were two, and only one committed adultery").[46]

For Augustine the point is that Lucretia was innocent in the rape and therefore did not merit the death penalty. Even in the unlikely event that she had secretly enjoyed her encoun-

---

[46] Aug., *de Civ. Dei* 1.19. Cf. I. Donaldson, *The Rapes of Lucretia: A Myth and its Transformation* (Oxford, 1982).

ter with Tarquin, she should still not have killed herself when she could have practiced penance instead. For Augustine it is wrong to add to the crime of another, such as rape, the crime of murdering a person, namely oneself. The commandment, "Thou shalt not kill," applies to any human being. As Augustine put it with epigrammatic force, *neque enim qui se occidit aliud quam hominem occidit* ("For he who kills himself kills no other than a man").[47]

This ringing denunciation of suicide brought Christianity firmly in line with the ethics of Graeco-Judaic philosophy. It constituted a formal and final repudiation of the old Roman way to a glorious death. In doing so it closed the door once and for all on voluntary martyrs, and from this time onward the ὁμολογητής or *confessor* represented an aspirant to martyrdom who was precluded from shedding his own blood. The old pre-Constantinian martyrs, the earliest in the Church's history, had responded to Roman ethical values and civic institutions that, by the time of Augustine, had already vanished in the Byzantine empire and were slowly fading in the Latin West. But in the Graeco-Roman world of the late first and second centuries the metamorphosis of traditional terms for witness and witnessing into an ideology of death to promote a cause had served as a powerful symbol of Greek culture adapted to the Roman empire. With the ultimate exclusion of suicide from that ideology Christian martyrdom was deprived of its most militant, its most Roman feature. But ironically it was that very feature that was conspicuously to survive in Islam, when the heirs of the prophet Muhammad ruled in the land where Jesus was crucified.

[47] Aug., *de Civ. Dei* 1.20, *ad fin.*

Appendix 1
Protomartyr

Stephen is traditionally designated the first martyr, πρωτο-μάρτυς. But in the earliest centuries of the Church this was by no means the case. In the account of the martyrs of Lyon in AD 177, as preserved by Eusebius in what is arguably an authentic document (see Appendix IV below), the first to advance to their deaths in the persecution are simply and plausibly called πρωτομάρτυρες (*HE* 5.1.11). There is no suggestion that the singular of the noun might describe the first of all martyrs in the history of Christianity.

The word does not appear in the New Testament. In the detailed narrative of Acts 7 on the stoning of Stephen those who witness the event are called οἱ μάρτυρες (7.58). At Acts 22.20 comes the notorious description of Stephen himself as a μάρτυς: ὅτε ἐξεχύννετο τὸ αἷμα Στεφάνου τοῦ μάρτυρός σου. The σου here refers to the Lord. Apart from the frequent and consistent use of μάρτυς in the New Testament in its usual sense of witness (and, in particular, at Acts 7.58), what Stephen actually did witness before he was stoned is obviously pertinent: εἰς τὸν οὐρανὸν εἶδεν δόξαν Θεοῦ καὶ Ἰησοῦν ἑστῶτα ἐκ δεξίων τοῦ Θεοῦ. He saw God with Jesus at His right hand. The most reasonable reading of τοῦ μάρτυρός σου in Acts 22.20 is therefore "witness of the Lord." Nothing in the New Testament implies that the word for witness meant martyr when those texts were written. The description of Jesus himself by John in Apoc. 1.5 and 3.14 as ὁ μάρτυς ὁ πιστός must be – and usually is – understood as "faithful witness."

Appendix 1

The earliest instances of Stephen as πρωτομάρτυς, meaning "first of all martyrs," appear in texts of the fourth century: Gregory of Nyssa, *Steph.* 2 (46.725B – misprinted C – Migne) and Epiphanius, *Pan.* 1.2, *Haer.* 25 (41.321A Migne); *Pan.* 3.1, *Haer.* 70.6 (42.348C Migne). But in this transitional and, it must be said, creative period others are also equipped with the title of protomartyr. The legendary Thecla is so characterized in the opening of her *Acta* and elsewhere (Isidore of Pelusium, *ep.* 1.160 [78.289C] and Evagrius, *HE* 3.8 [86.2612B Migne]). Jesus himself, who has a much better claim, is called πρωτομάρτυς by Gelasius of Cyzicus in the fifth century in his *HE* 2.19.26 (85.1280D Migne).

The word πρωτομάρτυς evidently did not appear until μάρτυς had already acquired the meaning of martyr. The Lyon *martyrium* implies that it was originally used to single out those courageous souls who went to their deaths first in a particular persecution. The recognition that someone in the early decades of the Church had to have been the first martyr of all seems to have been part of post-Constantinian theology, and for at least a century or so there was uncertainty as to who that person was – Stephen, Thecla, or Jesus himself.

Appendix 2
Ignatius and IV Maccabees

Perhaps the most remarkable thing about Ignatius of Antioch, as we know him from his letters, is that his zeal for death at the hands of the Roman authorities is wholly untouched by the language of martyrdom. As Charles Munier recently observed, "Ignace ne connaît pas encore les acceptions techniques des termes μάρτυς, μαρτύριον, pour désigner le témoignage sanglant; bien mieux, il ne connaît aucun terme réservé à cette signification."[1] Ignatius's career is assigned by Eusebius to the early second century (*HE* 3.36.2–4), and his sanguinary demise at Rome is put, not perhaps with complete accuracy, in AD 107 (*Chron.*). If μάρτυς had meant martyr at that time, Ignatius would undoubtedly have availed himself of the word.

Instead the bishop expresses the act of self-sacrifice in the Christian cause as an aspect of simply being a Christian (Χριστιανός), of striving to imitate Jesus (μιμητής), and of being a student of Jesus (μαθητής). These, as K. Bommes has shown,[2] are the periphrases by which Ignatius describes what was

---

[1] On the whole subject of Ignatius's enthusiasm for suffering, see K. Bommes, *Weizen Gottes. Untersuchungen zur Theologie des Martyriums bei Ignatius von Antiochien* (Cologne–Bonn, 1976); H. J. Vogt, "Ignatius von Antiochien. Das Leiden als Zeugnis und Heilsweg," in *Der Mensch in Grenzsituation*, ed. E. Olshausen (Stuggart, 1984), pp. 49–71. For a full and useful survey of opinions and publications, see Charles Munier, "Où en est la question d'Ignace d'Antioche? Bilan d'un siècle de recherches 1870–1988," *Aufstieg und Niedergang der römischen Welt* II 27.1 (1993), pp. 359–484, especially pp. 455–63. The citation from Munier is taken from p. 456.
[2] Bommes, *Weizen Gottes*.

later to be called a martyr. It is evident that none of these terms has that meaning as such. The sacrifice, of which Ignatius is enamoured, is not even a necessary aspect of those three categories, except perhaps for him.

Ignatius is often more comfortable and more explicit when he writes in metaphors. Among these the extraordinary formulations in his letter to the Romans (4–5) are the most celebrated – the food of beasts (θηρίων βορά), the wheat of God (σῖτος θεοῦ) to be ground up by the teeth of animals so that he can become the pure bread of Christ (καθαρὸς ἄρτος τοῦ Χριστοῦ). In this amazing passage, anticipating the deadly work of the animals at Rome, Ignatius calmly declares, Νῦν ἄρχομαι μαθητὴς εἶναι – a true student at last.

Some of Ignatius's metaphors are more prosaic. These have afforded scholars an opportunity to draw parallels with other texts. Othmar Perler was particularly diligent in looking for words that Ignatius shared with the author of the Fourth Book of Maccabees.[3] He cast his net so wide that he included a word (εὔλογος) that does not appear in ɪv Macc. at all, and he gave unwarranted emphasis to words of relative frequency and even banality in Greek of the imperial age (καλοκἀγαθία, ἀκόλουθος, εὔνοια, κατάλυσις). Perler dilated on the imagery of the athlete and competitive sport, as though this bound Ignatius with the author of ɪv Macc. instead of revealing both as children of their age.[4] And when Ignatius's use of the leopard as metaphor in Rom. 5.1 is compared with allusions to wild beasts in ɪv Macc. (even though no leopards are mentioned), Perler hears an echo of a Syrian homeland.[5]

Although later patristic writers, such as Ambrose, John

---

[3] O. Perler, "Das vierte Makkabäerbuch, Ignatius von Antiochien, und die ältesten Märtyrerberichte," *Revista di archeologia cristiana* 25 (1949), 47–72.

[4] Perler, "Das vierte Makkabäerbuch," pp. 49–51.

[5] Perler, "Das vierte Makkabäerbuch," p. 55: "Man ist versucht, die Quelle wiederum im 4 Makk. zu vermuten, umso mehr als das Bild bei Ignatius übertrieben scheint; galten doch die Leoparde, häufig aus Syrien stammend, als besonders grausam und wild."

Chrysostom, and Gregory of Nyssa, showed themselves, as Perler knew, well acquainted with IV Macc., there was little point in his stressing words from that Jewish document that are not to be found in the New Testament. When it was written IV Macc. reflected Hellenistic Judaism but hardly Christianity. Despite Perler's efforts, the work can neither be assigned to a date before Ignatius nor have provided a repertorium for the bishop's vocabulary. Already before Perler, André Dupont-Sommer had made an important case for a late Trajanic or Hadrianic date for IV Macc.,[6] and now van Henten has plausibly anchored the work a little later in the time of the earliest Christian martyrological texts.[7]

What the language of Ignatius and IV Macc. seems clearly to reflect is a common origin for both in the imperial Greek of Asia Minor.[8] This is not surprising for Ignatius, who wrote his letters there, but it is of greater interest for a Jewish narrative that has not normally been assigned a local habitation. Since Asia Minor, as I have argued in the foregoing chapters, was the homeland of the whole phenomenon of Christian martyrdom, these texts – one Christian and one Jewish – may be seen as repositories of enthusiasm for the subject before it was articulated in terms of "witnessing" (μαρτύριον).

One interesting and unusual lection that is common to both Ignatius and IV Macc. may help us to understand better the conceptualization of self-sacrifice on the eve of martyrdom as

[6] A. Dupont-Sommer, *Le quatrième livre des Machabées* (Paris, 1939).

[7] J. W. van Henten, "Datierung und Herkunft des vierten Makkabäerbuches," in *Tradition and Reinterpretation in Jewish and Early Christian Literature*, Essays in Honour of J. C. H. Lebram, ed. van Henten and de Jonge (Leiden, 1986), pp. 136–49.

[8] See the excellent discussion of IV Macc. in J. W. van Henten, "The Martyrs as Heroes of the Christian People. Some remarks on the continuity between Jewish and Christian martyrology, with pagan analogies," to appear in a volume on early Christian martyrdom, ed. Lamderigts, in the BETL series at Louvain. I am very grateful to the author for showing me (through the kind intercession of Peter Schäfer) a typescript of his valuable article in advance of publication. Particularly telling are van Henten's observations on the verb κηδεύω in IV Macc. in relation to pagan epitaphs in Phrygia and Lycia.

such. Ignatius makes reference four times to the idea of substituting one life for another as a justification for sacrificing oneself:

Eph. 21.1: Ἀντίψυχον ὑμῶν ἐγὼ καὶ ὧν ἐπέμψατε εἰς Θεοῦ τιμὴν εἰς Σμύρναν.

Smyrn. 10.2: Ἀντίψυχον ὑμῶν τὸ πνεῦμά μου καὶ τὰ δεσμά μου.

Polyc. 2.3: Κατὰ πάντα σου ἀντίψυχον ἐγὼ καὶ τὰ δεσμά μου.

Polyc. 6.1: Ἀντίψυχον ἐγὼ τῶν ὑποτασσομένων τῷ ἐπισκόπῳ, πρεσβυτέροις, διακόνοις.

Although the word ἀντίψυχος is not often found, its two appearances in ιν Macc. do not suffice to prove that Ignatius was drawing on those passages,[9] nor indeed that the author of ιν Macc. was drawing on Ignatius:

ιν Macc. 6.29: ἀντίψυχον αὐτῶν λάβε τὴν ἐμὴν ψύχην.

ιν Macc. 17.22: ὥσπερ ἀντίψυχον γεγονότας τῆς τοῦ ἔθνους ἁμαρτίας.

Before the Christian literature of the fourth century (Eusebius and Athanasius),[10] ἀντίψυχος appears only twice outside the letters of Ignatius and the text of ιν Macc., both times in pagan texts written by authors from Asia Minor. Lucian, from Samosata on the Euphrates, uses the word in the mid-second century in *Lexiph.* 10: ὥστε ἐν δεσμοῖς ὢν ὑπέβδυλλέ τε ὁ κακοδαίμων ὑπὸ τοῦ δέους καὶ πορδαλέος ἦν καὶ χρήματα ἀντίψυχα δεδόναι ἤθελεν.[11] Cassius Dio, from Nicaea in Bithynia, wrote in the third century in his *Roman History* (59.8.3) about a man who offered to give up his life and another who offered to fight as a gladiator if only Caligula would recover from an illness: ἀντὶ γὰρ τῶν χρημάτων ἃ

9 It is regrettable that Munier, in his survey published in 1993 (cited above, n. 1), can still assert (p. 461), "Ignace exprime la même idée [d'un sacrifice expiatoire] au moyen du terme ἀντίψυχος, qu'il emprunte vraisemblablement au ιν^e Livre des Maccabées."

10 Euseb., *Dem. Ev.* 1.10; Athan., *de incarn.* 9 (25.112B Migne).

11 Macleod's *OCT* edition reads ἔνδεσμος and πορδάλεος.

ἤλπιζον παρ' αὐτοῦ ὡς καὶ ἀντίψυχοί οἱ ἀποθανεῖν ἐθελήσαν-
τες λήψεσθαι, ἀποδοῦναι τὴν ὑπόσχεσιν ἠναγκάσθησαν, ἵνα μὴ
ἐπιορκήσωσι.

In Lucian the terrified prisoner wanted to pay χρήματα
ἀντίψυχα if someone would take his place. In Dio the two
hapless Romans thought that they would receive money by
offering to die (and were cruelly obliged to carry through on
their pledge when the emperor recovered). In both cases what
is at stake is payment to liberate another from impending
death. The allusion to the prisoner's chains in Lucian reminds
one of Ignatius in two of the places cited above, where he
conjoined τὰ δεσμά μου with his own person as part of the
exchange. The metaphor in Ignatius becomes perfectly clear
in the light of Lucian and Dio: he will free the Christians by
assuming their bondage and death. Ignatius is accepting
χρήματα ἀντίψυχα in spiritual coin.

Since this metaphor for substitution occurs, on present
evidence, only in the second and third centuries and only in
Asia Minor, it would appear to be another suggestive item in
the dossier for the emergence of martyrdom in that part of the
world. The testimony of Ignatius and Lucian together implies
that the social context for this metaphor (and the word ἀντίψυχος) was a local penal system in which a prisoner with
money could pay another to take his place.

Appendix 3
Great Sabbath

Two of the earliest martyr narratives, both of which appear to be substantially authentic, place their martyrdoms in Smyrna at a time described as "Great Sabbath":

Mart. Polycarpi:
>   8.1: ὄντος σαββάτου μεγάλου
>   21: σαββάτῳ μεγάλῳ (dated 23 February)

Mart. Pionii:
>   2: ἐνισταμένου σαββάτου μεγάλου (dated 23 February)
>   3.6: ἐγεμίσθη πᾶσα ἡ ἀγορὰ καὶ αἱ ὑπερῷαι στοαὶ
>   Ἑλλήνων τε καὶ Ἰουδαίων καὶ γυναικῶν· ἐσχόλαζον
>   γὰρ διὰ τὸ εἶναι μέγα σάββατον.

The interpretation of this festal date has long been a subject of controversy, as can be readily discerned from two recent and important discussions: W. Rordorf, "Zum Problem des Großen Sabbats im Polykarp- und Pioniosmartyrium," in *Pietas: Festschrift für Bernhard Kötting*, Jahrb. f. Ant. u. Christ. Ergänzungsbd. 8 (Münster, 1980), pp. 245–9; and P. Devos, "Μέγα Σάββατον chez Saint Epiphane," *Anal. Bolland.* 108 (1990), 293–306.

The reference has usually been taken to be to the Christian Sabbath, i.e. Sunday. Cf. L. Robert, *Le martyre de Pionios*, ed. G. W. Bowersock and C. P. Jones (Dumbarton Oaks, 1994), p. 50. But the earliest certain use of the expression in this sense is Epiphanius in the fourth century: *De exp. fid.* 24 (42.829C–D Migne), comparing the Jewish Sabbath (μικρὸν Σάββατον), διαναπαύεται ἐν τῷ μεγάλῳ σαββάτῳ ἀντὶ τοῦ μικροῦ σαββάτοῦ. In *Chron. Pasch.* 211 (92.516B Migne) Sunday (κυριακή) is distinguished from σάββατον: ἡμέρα δευτέρα τοῦ σαββάτου ("the next day after the Sabbath"). For John Chrysostom, *Hom. in Ps.* 145,2 (5.525D Migne), τὸ μέγα Σάββατον is precisely the day before Easter. This remains the meaning of "Great Sabbath" today in both the Greek Orthodox and Russian Orthodox liturgies: μέγα Σάββατον / dem. μεγάλο Σαββάτο and *velikaya Subbota*, extending from sundown on Friday until Saturday at midnight before Easter.

The crowds that attend the martyrdoms of Polycarp and Pionios at Smyrna imply that Greek pagans and Jews were on holiday at that time, and ἐσχόλαζον in *Mart. Pionii* 3.6 explicitly confirms this. Hence one must identify a period of time in which the whole community would be at leisure. Only the Roman authorities seem to be at work. The date of 23 February in both martyrdoms appears to be too early for the day before Easter. If it is accurate in both instances this must have been a time that the Roman government found useful for such cautionary proceedings. Some coincidence of Christian and Jewish holidays with a local one appears likely (Rordorf thought of the *Terminalia*). It is possible that Great Sabbath designated a festival season rather than a day. Certainly the Paschal sense of Great Sabbath extends well over a single day. The word σάββατον had, as early as Clement (*Strom.* 4.3), a metaphorical meaning of repose and self-restraint. It is this meaning which Devos finds in an extended form in Epiphanius ("le Christ en personne, considéré comme nous 'faisant repos' des fautes"). He promises a study of the expression in the martyrdoms of Polycarp and Pionios, to which we must look forward eagerly.

If Great Sabbath were more than a day and came soon to be associated with Easter (as it was to be later in its more restricted sense), perhaps Lent is at issue here – in conjunction with a local festival. The first definite indication of the celebration of Lent does not occur until a letter of Athanasius in 330, but the Byzantine expression "Great Lent," in contradistinction to other lesser Lents (before the Nativity, for example), suggests the possibility of a similar sense of μέγα Σάββατον before the fourth century. For the history of Lent, the *Oxford Dictionary of Byzantium* (1991), vol. 2, pp. 1025–6, provides the basic facts.

Appendix 4
Asia, Aphrodisias, and the *Lyon* Martyrium

Nearly two decades ago I queried the extraordinary prescript of the great letter, preserved by Eusebius, concerning the martyrdom at Lyon in the year AD 177.[1] The letter, clearly full of many authentic details concerning the martyrdom, begins with a prescript containing a striking formulation of the home territory of the recipients: οἱ ἐν Βιέννῃ καὶ Λουγδούνῳ τῆς Γαλλίας παροικοῦντες δοῦλοι Χριστοῦ τοῖς κατὰ τὴν Ἀσίαν καὶ Φρυγίαν τὴν αὐτὴν τῆς ἀπολυτρώσεως ἡμῖν πίστιν καὶ ἐλπίδα ἔχουσιν ἀδελφοῖς. The conjunction of Asia and Phrygia seemed odd, inasmuch as Phrygia was an integral part of Asia in normal second-century usage, although a few texts of apparently later date displayed such phrasing as "Asia and Phrygia," "Asia and Lydia," or "Asia and Caria." Such formulations appeared to reflect the time of Eusebius himself and the provincial organization instituted under the Tetrarchy, when regions such as Phrygia or Caria became independent provinces. The prescript seemed therefore less likely to be authentic than most of the body of the letter. But it is now evident, in the light of the materials assembled here, that this apparent anomaly is, on the contrary, a striking guarantee of the authenticity of the prescript. We are, after all, in the reign of Marcus Aurelius, and the *martyrium* joins its brethren among the earliest Martyr Acts, notably the accounts of Poly-

---

[1] Euseb., *HE* 5.1. See G. W. Bowersock, *Les martyrs de Lyon*, colloques internationaux du CNRS – no. 575 (Paris, 1978), pp. 249–56.

carp, Perpetua, and Pionios, as a substantially contemporary document.

The issue must, however, be approached by a circuitous route through the tangled history of rival claims of the cities of western Asia Minor for preeminence and glory. The ample testimony of inscriptions and coins from the cities of Asia has long since illustrated this enthusiasm for what has seemed to modern scholars (and indeed to the Romans themselves) petty and vainglorious titles. As T. R. S. Broughton wrote in his contribution of 1938: "Rivalry among several of the larger and more ambitious cities became intense, led to a great deal of wasteful display, and by the end of the second century resulted in a general increase in honorific titles until they bore little relation to the relative station and importance of the city. The virus spread into smaller cities."[2] Even at the end of the first century AD the Greek orator and philosopher, Dio Chrysostom, chided the citizens of Nicomedia in Bithynia for their excessive interest in honorific titles, which, he said, were known in the Roman world as "the failings of the Greeks" (Ἑλληνικὰ ἁμαρτήματα).[3] It is easy for modern scholars to adopt the supercilious tone of the Romans; and yet, as Simon Price pointed out in his book on the imperial cult, to do so would seriously damage our understanding of the social and economic dynamics of Asia Minor.[4]

The report of Dio Chrysostom should not lead us to believe that the Roman administration considered these honorific titles of no importance. Inscriptions of the period can leave us in no doubt that a long and complex diplomatic procedure

[2] T. R. S. Broughton, "Roman Asia," in vol. 4 of *An Economic Survey of Ancient Rome*, ed. Tenney Frank (Baltimore, 1938), pp. 741–4. Much of the argument in this appendix was presented in 1990 in the inaugural Broughton Lecture at the University of North Carolina (Chapel Hill), in the presence of Professor Broughton.

[3] L. Robert, "La titulature de Nicée et de Nicomédie: la gloire et la haine," *HSCP* 81 (1977), 1–39 [*Opera Minora Selecta*, hereafter *OMS*, 6.211–49].

[4] S. R. F. Price, *Rituals and Power: The Roman Imperial Cult in Asia Minor* (Cambridge, 1984).

was required of any city that wished to be considered for a special title. No title could be assumed on the coinage or in the epigraphy of a city without the formal authorization of the Roman government. This meant that an ambitious city had to send a group of citizens on an embassy to the Roman authorities of the province and then, perhaps, even to Rome in order to persuade the senate and the emperor of its merits. Nicaea, for example, proudly proclaimed itself on its city gate as a metropolis κατὰ τὰ κρίματα τῶν αὐτοκρατόρων καὶ τῆς ἱερᾶς συνκλήτου.[5] At Sardis a similar phrase is found when it boasts that it has two temples of the imperial cult in the city κατὰ τὰ δόγματα τῆς ἱερᾶς συνκλήτου.[6] The titles that were the object of this extensive diplomatic activity were essentially three in number: "metropolis," "first city" (πρώτη πόλις), and νεωκό-ρος (or "temple guardian"). The last category designated those cities with a temple of the imperial cult, and those with more than one were entitled to declare themselves νεωκόρος twice or even thrice.

It is obvious on the face of it that being a metropolis and being a first city are rather similar distinctions, but they were not altogether trivial since they indicated the placement of city representatives in ceremonial events where the cities of the province were on display. The orator Aelius Aristides alludes to the phenomenon of πρωτεῖα in memorable lines:

> Come let me describe those cities which now vie for first place and which are the greatest source of strife, no more through their fault, as I should say, than through that of all the other people who have taken sides with them. For everyone wishes to revile the other cities as much as he can on behalf of the city to which he happens to be favorably disposed.[7]

---

5 Sencer Şahin, *Bithynische Studien/Bithynia Incelemeleri* (Cologne, 1978), pp. 18–19 and 85–6.

6 *Sardis* VII.1, no. 63: πρώτης Ἑλλάδος καὶ μητροπόλεως τῆς Ἀσίας καὶ Λυδίας ἁπάσης καὶ δὶς νεωκόρου τῶν Σεβαστῶν κατὰ τὰ δόγματα τῆς ἱερᾶς συνκλή-του. For the formulae, see also nos. 64 and 67–70.

7 Aristid., *Orat.* 23.12 (Keil).

Metropolis was the more exclusive category, and Dio Chrysostom even tried to resolve the differences between Nicomedia and Nicaea by suggesting that, although only one could be a metropolis in the late first century AD, both could enjoy the title of first city or πρώτη πόλις.[8] The controversies over titles became even more intense and complex in the generations after Dio Chrysostom, as can be seen in a famous letter of Antoninus Pius in which the emperor attempted to mediate the not inconsiderable claims of Ephesus, Pergamum, and Smyrna at the same time. Pius's letter was obviously of such general interest that no less than three copies of it have turned up amid the remains of Roman Ephesus.[9]

One reason, insufficiently appreciated, for the alarming growth in the competition for titles in the second century AD was the apparently deliberate change in Roman policy toward the status of metropolis. The word meant, of course, simply "mother city," and unofficially it could be used by any place that had dispatched colonies abroad. Tyre in Phoenicia could boast of its glorious past in colonizing the West by proclaiming itself a mother city.[10] Similarly, Miletus, which was never an official metropolis recognized by the Roman government, could nonetheless call itself the "metropolis of many and great cities in Pontus and Egypt and many other places in the inhabited world."[11] But the official title metropolis, as it appeared on coins and in the formal titulature of a city, was strictly controlled by the Roman government. In the first century AD it was evidently limited, after petition through diplomatic channels, to one city in a province. That would naturally be the principal or capital city. Dio Chrysostom, in his attempt to mediate between Nicomedia and Nicaea,

[8] Dio Chrys., *Orat.* 38.39.
[9] *Inschr. Kleinasiens,* hereafter *IK, Eph.* 1489, 1489A, 1490 (*SIG*³ 849).
[10] *Inschr. Didyma,* ed. Rehm, no. 151.
[11] *CIG* 2878, Le Bas-Waddington, *Inscr. grecques et latines recueillies en Asie Mineure,* no. 212.

reflected this restriction when he made his paradoxical suggestion that, although only one city could be metropolis, two might perhaps be first. As late as the reign of Nerva, the city of Beroea in Macedonia achieved by diplomacy the right to maintain sole possession of the title of metropolis against the claims of another, rival city, presumably Pella. An inscription refers to the privilege of displaying the title as τὸ τῆς μητρο-πόλεως ἀξίωμα ("the distinction of metropolis").[12]

There is, in fact, no certain violation of the principle of one official metropolis per province in the Roman empire before the reign of Hadrian. From that reign onward multiple metropolises begin to appear in the various provinces of the eastern empire. A curious notice in the biography of Hadrian in the *Augustan History* seems to reflect the emperor's interest in distributing the title of metropolis more widely. There it is reported that Hadrian contemplated at one stage separating Syria from Phoenice so that Antioch would no longer be the metropolis of so many cities. In other words, what seems to underlie this proposal is the old principle of one metropolis per province, which would compel the separation of a single province into two in order to create two metropolises in place of one. But Hadrian, as the epigraphic material proves, obviously and wisely preferred to lift the restriction rather than to carve up the eastern provinces into increasingly smaller units in order to honor more cities.[13]

In many cases it seems clear that Hadrian did, however, take into account the natural regional divisions of the provinces, divisions which themselves could be represented in Greek unofficially by the word ἐπαρχεῖαι. In an inscription of AD 119–20 at Jerash, at the beginning of Hadrian's reign, Antioch could be called the metropolis of the four Syrian ἐπαρχεῖαι, which we might translate loosely as "provincial

---

[12] *SEG* 17.315 (*Bull. épig.* 1971.400).
[13] G. W. Bowersock, "Hadrian and Metropolis," *Bonner Historia–Augusta–Colloquium* 1982/1983 (Bonn, 1985), pp. 75–88, with reference to *HA*, Hadr. 14.1.

regions."[14] Not much later, when additional metropolises are established in Syria, the new cities with the title seem to represent those very ἐπαρχεῖαι over which Antioch had formerly presided. These are Samosata in Commagene, Tyre in Phoenice, and Damascus in Coele Syria, all in addition to Antioch itself with its dominant role in the limestone massif of the Belus. We have thus four metropolises for the four ἐπαρχεῖαι.

By the reign of Antoninus Pius the transformation that took place under Hadrian becomes fully documented in several eastern provinces.[15] In Asia both Ephesus and Pergamum are now metropolises, in Bithynia both Nicaea and Nicomedia, in Pontus the cities of Amaseia, Neo-Caesarea, and Nicopolis; and in Lycia no fewer than five cities enjoyed the title of metropolis. These are Xanthos, Patara, Tlos, Myra, and Telmessos. By the end of the century even some tribal units have their own metropolises, such as the Moccadênoi of Asia. Antoninus Pius's letter implies that the new liberality of the second century in bestowing the title of metropolis had been expected to ease the tensions between cities, although it had obviously not always achieved that objective. In Asia in particular, the quarrels among Ephesus, Pergamum, and Smyrna left completely out of account the claims of the great regional divisions of the province, such as Lydia, Phrygia, and Caria. This concentration on the problems of the coastal cities of Asia at the expense of the interior was bound to cause problems sooner or later. As things turned out, it was sooner.

A remarkable new title "first metropolis of Caria" turned up on two inscriptions from the facade of the temple of Apollo at Klaros. Jeanne and Louis Robert discovered these texts among the many hundreds of inscriptions along the Sacred Way at Klaros during the course of their excavations there in the early

[14] C. B. Welles, in C. M. Kraehling, *Gerasa: City of the Decapolis* (New Haven, 1938), p. 399, no. 53, ll. 4–5 [also *SEG* 7.847].
[15] See documentation provided in Bowersock, "Hadrian and Metropolis."

1950s. In an article in 1957 Louis Robert made reference to the phrase "first metropolis of Caria" in an inscription recording a delegation to Apollo of Klaros from the city of Aphrodisias: Ἀφροδεισίων τῆς πρώτης μητροπόλεως τῆς Καρίας.[16] Inasmuch as the hundreds of texts recording delegations to the oracle mention magistrates at the shrine, whose dates can be determined within a range of one or two years, it was possible to fix the designation of Aphrodisias to the decade of 170 to 180. I can report here, through the courtesy of Mme Robert, that his own notes on one of the two texts deduce a more precise date of 171–172. The title is utterly unexampled and unexpected.

Several texts from Aphrodisias much later – in the fourth century AD – show the city as a metropolis of Caria at the time when there was a Diocletianic province that bore the name Caria.[17] In the previous century, the third century AD, we now know, thanks to the excellent researches of Charlotte Roueché on the new inscriptions from Aphrodisias, that, as early as the time of Philip the Arab in the middle of the century, a new province of Phrygia and Caria had come into existence, carved out of the old province of Asia.[18] But during the lifetime of the province of Phrygia and Caria, Aphrodisias is not yet actually attested as a metropolis (although it is more than likely to have been one). For the decade of the 170s, when it has always been assumed that the province of Asia was of the size that had been traditional since the beginning of the empire, a title such as first metropolis of Caria is particularly surprising.

---

[16] *REG* 70 (1957), 370, n. 4, = *OMS* 3.1487, n. 4. In this reference L. Robert cites only one of the two inscriptions of Aphrodisias as "metropolis of Caria." Both are unpublished.

[17] C. Roueché, *Aphrodisias in Late Antiquity* (London, 1989), p. 45, no. 23 and p. 56, no. 32.

[18] C. Roueché, "Rome, Asia and Aphrodisias in the Third Century," *JRS* 71 (1981), 103–20 (esp. 118, n. 99). Cf. *Images of Authority*, Papers presented to Joyce Reynolds, Suppl. vol. 16 of Cambridge Philological Society (Cambridge, 1989), p. 218 and n. 99 (on pp. 226–7).

For one thing, Aphrodisias lies at the very northern edge of Caria; and, while it might seem a suitable metropolis for a province of Phrygia and Caria together, it would appear to be somewhat oddly situated for a metropolis in Caria alone. For those few scholars who have reflected on the institutional organization of Caria in this period, Stratonicea further south seemed a much better candidate. It is more centrally located, and there is one inscription in which it is named simply "metropolis of Caria."[19] It was to this evidence that Charlotte Roueché had recourse when she faced the problem in a footnote to her excellent article on the third-century province of Phrygia and Caria. She noted that the title metropolis was used of Aphrodisias at Klaros in the 170s and then did not appear again until the fourth century. "Stratonicea," she wrote, "is more widely attested as metropolis" – although it must be said it is attested only once, which is scarcely more widely – and "had played a more important part in the history of Caria, and is more centrally located in the province."[20] This inscription from Stratonicea requires a closer look.

The text is a decree of the people in honor of a priest of the imperial cult and his wife. In the second line the city is called autochthonous and metropolis of Caria, τῆς αὐτόχθονος καὶ μητροπόλεως τῆς Καρίας. The original editor, Hatzfeld, working from a copy of Cousin, had deduced a date for this text in the latter part of the first century AD entirely on the basis of the family names. Hatzfeld suggested a genealogy of families attested in inscriptions of the city, although he recognized perfectly well that this was the most fragile of reconstructions. What we now know about restrictions on the title metropolis in the first century AD would naturally make such a dating suspect in any case. But, fortunately, archaeologists who have reexamined the temple of the imperial cult at Stratonicea have concluded that it cannot be dated with any

[19] *IK, Stratonikeia* no. 15 (*SEG* 4.262).
[20] Roueché, "Rome, Asia and Aphrodisias," p. 118, n. 99.

probability before the reign of Hadrian. This means that the inscription in honor of priests of the cult must certainly be after that date.

Apart from the text at Klaros, there is no other attestation of the title metropolis for the region of Caria in either the second or the third centuries AD. Since Aphrodisias calls itself the first metropolis, and Stratonicea is simply a metropolis, we must naturally ask whether or not these two inscriptions are actually contemporaneous. In fact, the editor of the inscriptions of Stratonicea in the Cologne corpus of inscriptions of Asia Minor, Çetin Şahin, has now proposed a new stemma for the family of the priests in the inscription we are considering. Without regard to the problem of the title of metropolis, he has created a series of four generations from the time in which these priests received the family name of Flavius.[21] Hence the priests would be pretty squarely located in the period of Marcus Aurelius, exactly the period indicated by the date on the Klaros text. Accordingly there are converging reasons for removing the Stratonicea text from the first century AD and placing it, in all probability, in the 160s or 170s.

Our attention is thus directed to the time before, during, and just after the Parthian wars of Lucius Verus. This would appear to be the time of the separation of the territory of Caria into an independently recognized unit with its own metropolis. Such a reorganization at this date can hardly be an accident, and it can be satisfactorily integrated into a pattern of administrative changes that reflect the imperial arrangements for conduct of the war. In about 165, on the eve of Lucius Verus's expedition, the province of Bithynia-Pontus, through which lay an important communication route with the East, was removed from the control of the senate. Since the days of Augustus, Bithynia-Pontus had been administered by a praetorian proconsul in the apportionment of provinces

---

[21] See Çetin Şahin in *IK, Stratonikeia*, on no. 15.

allotted to the senate as opposed to those in the power of the emperor. Obviously in order to ensure a tighter control of the area because of its strategic importance, Marcus Aurelius brought the province into the orbit of his own imperial provinces, and he repaid the senate by transferring from the imperial administration the province of Lycia-Pamphylia, which now became a senatorial possession. This trade, which is clearly reflected in the epigraphic evidence for the governors of the two areas, was also recorded by Cassius Dio, although it has been transmitted to us in a miserable and misplaced Byzantine excerpt.[22] Nonetheless, it is clear that Dio recognized that the emperor intended to maintain the balance between senatorial and imperial provinces when he took over Bithynia-Pontus. Other rearrangements in Asia Minor at this time may also be expected in connection with the Parthian campaign. The sudden emergence of Caria as some kind of distinct administrative unit can best be explained in this way.

A number of supporting documents tend to reinforce the notion that the interior of Asia was reorganized so as to give new prominence to the traditional ethnic regions of Anatolia. Let us now consider several problematic cases that have never been brought together for comparison before. In the light of what we have deduced about Caria, they acquire an unexpected significance.

First an inscription from Hierapolis in Asia, not far away from Aphrodisias but already on the borders of Phrygia: the text honors a certain Publius Aelius Zeuxidemus Aristus Zeno, whose father had been a high priest of Asia and whose son was to be the celebrated sophist Aelius Antipater.[23] Since the father probably received his Roman citizenship at the hands

---

[22] D. Magie, *Roman Rule in Asia Minor* (Princeton, 1950), I.663 and II.1533 (but cf. *PIR*², L 231 on Licinius Priscus).

[23] *IGR* IV 819, συνήγορο[ν τ]οῦ ἐν Φρυγί[ᾳ ταμ]ιείου [καὶ] τοῦ ἐν ᾿Ασ[ίᾳ]. Cf. H.-G. Pflaum, *Les carrières procuratoriennes équestres* 1 (1960), p. 550, no. 205.

of Hadrian and the son was among the most important intellectuals of the time of Septimius Severus, it is apparent that
the career of Zeuxidemus Aristus Zeno must fall roughly in
the time of Marcus Aurelius. The inscription from Hierapolis
records that he was an *advocatus fisci* in *both* Phrygia *and* Asia.
This is a surprising item, since hitherto any post in Phrygia
would have constituted employment *within* the province of
Asia. The correlation of the two in conjunction can only mean,
as Pflaum observed, that at this time, under the reign of
Marcus Aurelius, there must have been two distinct treasuries
in the province of Asia – one for Phrygia and one for Asia
proper.

Next let us turn to the testimony in three inscriptions for the
procuratorial career of one Q. Cosconius Fronto who, among
a mass of financial posts in the empire, is recorded to have
administered the five per cent tax on inheritances *per Asiam,
Lyciam, Phrygiam, Galatiam.*[24] Once again we have the curious
phenomenon of Phrygia's being registered separately and in
parallel with Asia, even though one would have thought that
Phrygia was inside of Asia. Cosconius Fronto concluded his
busy career with an equestrian governorship of Sardinia, a
province which was entrusted to the equestrians in the time of
Commodus. To determine how soon after the reassignment of
Sardinia to equestrians Fronto undertook this responsibility,
we can have recourse to his prior procuratorial service, identified as service under Augusti, that is to say joint emperors.
Pflaum opted for Septimius Severus and Caracalla, but
equally possible, and I now believe more probable, are Marcus
Aurelius and Lucius Verus. We would thus have another
example of Phrygia as a procuratorial unit independent from
Asia.

Another remarkable text is an inscription from Phrygia itself

---

[24] *CIL* x, 7583 (Sardinia), 7584 (Cagliari, where *Pamphyliam* appears in the place
of *Asiam*), 7860 (Sardinia). See, on these texts, H.-G. Pflaum, *Les carrières
procuratoriennes équestres* 2 (1960), p. 706, no. 264.

that records the procuratorial career of a freedman of the emperor, a certain M. Aurelius Marcio.[25] Among his various financial posts is the surprising procuratorship of *provincia Phrygia*. The only clue we have to the date of this man's career is his name, Marcus Aurelius Augusti libertus Marcio, but that is good enough in the context of the other evidence we are deploying here. Yet again we clearly have an independent procuratorial district of Phrygia in, it would appear, the days of Marcus Aurelius.

From Sardis come several epigraphic attestations of an extraordinary title for that city at a date that has conventionally been assumed, after the judgment of the original editors, to be in the third century.[26] The city is called πρώτης Ἑλλάδος καὶ μητροπόλεως τῆς Ἀσίας καὶ Λυδίας ἁπάσης καὶ δὶς νεωκόρου τῶν Σεβαστῶν κατὰ τὰ δόγματα τῆς ἱερᾶς συνκλήτου. Here too we find the same curious phenomenon of an ethnically defined territory, namely Lydia, separated out from Asia, even though it is part of the province of Asia as we know it. The third-century date of the inscription was entirely based on the belief that Sardis did not receive its second neocorate, which is recorded in this text, until the very end of the second century. (It first appears on coins in the time of Clodius Albinus.) But thirty-six years ago, in a revelation typical of this ever growing field, an inscription turned up in the Sardis excavations that completely overthrew this dating of Sardis's second neocorate. On a statue base in honor of none other than Lucius Verus himself the city proudly displays its second neocorate: Αὐτοκράτορα Καίσαρα Αὐρ. Ἀντωνῖνον Οὐῆρον Σεβαστὸν ἡ β´ νεωκόρος Σαρδιανῶν πόλις.[27] Hence already in the 160s Sardis possessed that honor and perhaps even received it from that emperor. The implications of this discovery for the title of the city as

---

[25] *ILS* 1477.   [26] *Sardis* vii.1, no. 63.

[27] *Bull. épig.* 1962.290 [G. M. A. Hanfmann, *Archaeology* 12 (1959), pp. 57–8; *BASOR* 1960, pp. 7–10], found in 1958.

reflected in inscriptions that had long since been known have never been drawn. They mean quite unambiguously that this title of *neôkoros* for the second time must no longer be reserved to the third century. It is precisely a title of the time of Marcus and Lucius. In other words we are once more in the period of the Parthian wars, when we find again the separation of Asia from a part of itself. In this case we have Asia and Lydia.

When all these documents are taken together, we are compelled to acknowledge that in the fifteen years or so between 165 and 180, when Marcus died, the interior parts of the province of Asia were reorganized and given a separate identity according to their traditional ethnic character. Caria, Lydia, and Phrygia are all individually recognizable. They can be seen to be administered, at least within the procuratorial system, by administrators who are distinct from those in other parts of Asia. This arrangement undoubtedly permitted a much closer control over the movement of supplies, funds, and even troops through the Anatolian high roads to the east by way of the Maeander Valley, through the borders of Caria and Phrygia as well as by way of Sardis further north. There is no reason to think that these regions were made totally independent provinces; but, if Phrygia could be called a *provincia*, as it is in the inscription of the freedman Marcio, it is not unlikely that Caria, Lydia, and Phrygia felt themselves equally distinct (rather like Quebec in Canada). Hence we may now understand the appearance of metropolises for at least one of these regions. By a fortunate accident of survival we can see that there were even two metropolises in Caria, Stratonicea and Aphrodisias, and that Aphrodisias had the precedence by being named the first metropolis of Caria. That latter city may have been farther from the heartland of Caria, but it was much nearer to the main road to the east.

What is so extraordinary in the arrangements that come gradually into view, as we try to understand the Klaros inscription that attests this first metropolis of Caria, is the parallel between the tentative arrangements of Lucius Verus and Marcus Aurelius and the actual provincial arrangements that took shape in the third century and later under Diocletian and the Tetrarchs. We can observe already in the second century, for good prudential reasons, the breaking up of larger provinces into smaller units, and the Roman government's exploitation of the system of honorific titles in the stabilizing of the newly fragmented systems. The creation of smaller local units of administration allowed for the natural proliferation of local pride and, at the same time, the expression of regional autonomies that had been forcibly suppressed in the old traditional province of Asia.

That Marcus and Lucius should have anticipated all this and provided a kind of trial run for the province of Caria and Phrygia that subsequently took shape in the mid third century, to say nothing of the fragmented Asia Minor that emerged later still under the Tetrarchs, is a tribute to their astuteness and originality. So when we look again at the prescript to the *martyrium* of Lyon, it is amply revealed as a precious document of its time, AD 177. What once appeared to be a reflection of the work of the Tetrarchs and the age of Eusebius, who preserved the document, emerges as another proof of a prescient anticipation of those later arrangements in the epoch of the Antonines.

Select bibliography

Anderson, G., *The Second Sophistic* (London, 1993)

Barnes, T. D., "Pre-Decian *Acta Martyrum*," *Journal of Theological Studies* 19 (1968), 509–31

Tertullian (Oxford, 1971)

Bauer, W. K. and B. Aland, *Wörterbuch zum Neuen Testament*, 6th edn (Berlin, 1988)

Baumeister, T., *Die Anfänge der Theologie des Martyriums* (Münster, 1980)

Bommes, K., *Weizen Gottes. Untersuchungen zur Theologie des Martyriums bei Ignatius von Antiochien* (Cologne–Bonn, 1976)

Bowersock, G. W., *Greek Sophists in the Roman Empire* (Oxford, 1969)

"Les églises de Lyon et de Vienne: relations avec l'Asie," *Les martyrs de Lyon*, colloques internationaux du CNRS – no. 575 (Paris, 1978), pp. 249–56

"Hadrian and Metropolis," *Bonner Historia–Augusta–Colloquium* 1982/1983 (Bonns, 1985), pp. 75–88

Fiction as History: Nero to Julian, Sather Lectures (California, 1994)

Broughton, T. R. S., "Roman Asia," *An Economic Survey of Ancient Rome*, ed. Tenney Frank, vol. 4 (Baltimore, 1938)

Brox, Norbert, *Zeuge und Märtyrer: Untersuchungen zur frühchristlichen Zeugnis-Terminologie* (Munich, 1961)

Cartledge, P., P. Millett, and S. Todd (eds.), *Nomos: Essays in Athenian Law, Politics and Society* (Cambridge, 1990)

Clarke, G. W., *The Octavius of Marcus Minucius Felix* (New York, 1974)

The Letters of St. Cyprian, vol. 1 (New York, 1984); vol. 4 (1989)

Coleman, Kathleen M., "Fatal Charades: Roman Executions Staged as Mythological Enactments," *JRS* 80 (1990), 44–73

Coles, Revel A., *Reports of Proceedings in Papyri*, Papyrologica Bruxellensia 4 (Brussels, 1966)

Select bibliography

Dehandschutter, Boudewijn, "The *Martyrium Polycarpi*: A Century of Research," *Aufstieg und Niedergang der römischen Welt* II.27.1 (1993), pp. 485–522

Delehaye, H., "Martyr et confesseur," *Analecta Bollandiana* 39 (1921), 20–49

Les passions des martyrs et les genres littéraires (Brussels, 1921)

de Ste Croix, G. E. M., "Why Were the Early Christians Persecuted?," *Past and Present* no. 26 (1963), 6–38

Devos, P., "Μέγα Σάββατον chez Saint Épiphane," *Analecta Bollandiana* 108 (1990), 293–306

Dillon, J. M., *The Middle Platonists* (London, 1977)

Dodds, E. R., *Pagan and Christian in an Age of Anxiety* (Cambridge, 1965)

Donaldson, I., *The Rapes of Lucretia: A Myth and its Transformation* (Oxford, 1982)

Döring, K., *Exemplum Socratis* (Wiesbaden, 1979)

Doughty, C., *Travels in Arabia Deserta*, 3rd edn (New York, 1921)

Dupont-Sommer, A., *Le quatrième livre des Machabées* (Paris, 1939)

Durckheim, E., *Le suicide*, 3rd edn (Paris, 1930)

Frankfurter, David, "The Cult of the Martyrs in Egypt before Constantine," *Vigiliae Christianae* 48 (1994), 25–47

Frend, W. H. C., *Martyrdom and Persecution in the Early Church* (Blackwell, 1965)

Griffin, M. T., *Seneca: A Philosopher in Politics* (Oxford, 1976)

Grisé, Y., *Le suicide dans la Rome antique* (Montreal/Paris, 1983)

Habicht, Chr., 2. *Makkabäerbuch, Jüdische Schriften aus hellenistisch-römischer Zeit*, vol. 1 (Gütersloh, 1976)

Hanfmann, G. M. A., "Socrates and Christ," *Harvard Studies in Classical Philology* 60 (1951), 205–33

Hirzel, R., "Der Selbstmord," *Archiv für Religionswissenschaft* 11 (1908), 75–104, 243–84, 417–76 (reprinted Darmstadt, 1966)

Holford-Strevens, L., *Aulus Gellius* (London, 1988)

Knopf, R., G. Krüger and T. Ruhbach, *Ausgewählte Märtyrerakten* (Tübingen, 1965)

Kraehling, C. M., *Geresa: City of the Decapolis* (New Haven, 1938)

Lane, E. W., *An Arabic–English Lexicon* (London, 1872)

Lane Fox, Robin, *Pagans and Christians* (New York, 1987)

Magie, D., *Roman Rule in Asia Minor* (Princeton, 1950)

McManners, J. (ed.), *Oxford History of Christianity* (Oxford, 1990)

Munier, Charles, "Où en est la question d'Ignace d'Antioche? Bilan d'un siècle de recherches 1870–1988," *Aufstieg und Niedergang der römischen Welt* II.27.1 (1993), pp. 359–484

Musurillo, H., *Acts of the Pagan Martyrs* (Oxford, 1954)

Nutton, V., "Herodes and Gordian," *Latomus* 29 (1970), 725

Pagels, E., *Adam, Eve, and the Serpent* (New York, 1988)

Perler, O., "Das vierte Makkabäerbuch, Ignatius von Antiochien, und die ältesten Märtyrerberichte," *Revista di archeologia cristiana* 25 (1949), 47–72

Potter, D., "Martyrdom and Spectacle," in *Theater and Society in the Classical World*, ed. R. Scodel (Ann Arbor, 1993)

Price, S. R. F., *Rituals and Power: The Roman Imperial Cult in Asia Minor* (Cambridge, 1984)

Robert, Louis, *Les gladiateurs dans l'Orient grec* (Paris, 1940)

"La titulature de Nicée et de Nicomédie: la gloire et la haine," *HSCP* 81 (1977), 1–39 [= *Opera Minora Selecta*, 6.211–49]

"Une vision de Perpétue martyre à Carthage en 203," *Comptes rendus de l'Acad. des Inscr. et Belles-Lettres* (1982), 228–76 [= *Opera Minora Selecta*, 5.791–839]

Le martyre de Pionios, ed. G. W. Bowersock, and C. P. Jones (Dumbarton Oaks, 1994)

Rordorf, W., "Zum Problem des Großen Sabbats im Polykarp- und Pioniosmartyrium," *Pietas: Festschrift für Bernhard Kötting*, Jahrb. f. Ant. u. Christ. Ergänzungsbd. 8 (Münster, 1980), pp. 245–9

Roueché, C., "Rome, Asia and Aphrodisias in the Third Century," *JRS* 71 (1981), 103–20

Aphrodisias in Late Antiquity (London, 1989)

"Floreat Perge," *Images of Authority*, Papers presented to Joyce Reynolds, Suppl. vol. 16 of Cambridge Philological Society (Cambridge, 1989), pp. 205–28

Safrai, S., "Martyrdom in the Teachings of the Tannaim," in T. C. de Kruijf and H.v.d. Sandt, *Sjaloom* (Arnhem, 1983), pp. 145–64

Şahin, Sencer, *Bithynische Studien/Bithynia Incelemeleri* (Cologne, 1978)

Schmitt-Pantel, Pauline (ed.), *A History of Women in the West*, vol. 1 (Cambridge, Mass., 1992)

Shaw, B. D., "The Passion of Perpetua," *Past and Present* no. 139 (1993), 3–45

Select bibliography

Simon, M., *Verus Israël: étude sur les relations entre Chrétiens et Juifs dans l'Empire romain* (Paris, 1948; with supplement 1964)

Stadter, P. A., *Plutarch's Historical Methods* (Cambridge, Mass., 1965)

Thomasson, B., *Laterculi Praesidum* I (Göteborg, 1984)

van Henten, J. W. (ed.), *Die Entstehung der jüdischen Martyrologie* (Leiden, 1989)

"Datierung und Herkunft des vierten Makkabäerbuches," *Tradition and Reinterpretation in Jewish and Early Christian Literature*, Essays in Honour of J. C. H. Lebram, ed. van Henten and de Jonge (Leiden, 1986), pp. 136–49

"The Martyrs as Heroes of the Christian People. Some remarks on the continuity between Jewish and Christian martyrology, with pagan analogies" (forthcoming in a volume on early Christian martyrdom, ed. Lamderigts, in the BETL series, Louvain)

van Hooff, A., *From Autothanasia to Suicide: Self-Killing in Classical Antiquity* (London, 1990)

Vogt, H. J., "Ignatius von Antiochien. Das Leiden als Zeugnis und Heilsweg," *Der Mensch in Grenzsituation*, ed. E. Olshausen (Stuttgart, 1984), pp. 49–71

von Campenhausen, H., *Die Idee des Martyriums in der alten Kirche* (Göttingen, 1936)

Wirszubski, Ch., *Libertas as a Political Idea at Rome during the Late Republic and Early Principate* (Cambridge, 1960)

Wyrwa, Dietmar, *Die christliche Platonaneignung in den Stromateis des Clemens von Alexandrien* (Berlin, 1983)

Index

Index

Index

Syria, 61, 78, 89

Tarquin, 74
Telmessos, 90
Terminalia, 83
Tertullian, 2, 17, 18, 20, 36, 39, 54–6, 63,
   64, 65, 66, 73
testis, 19, 69
Thecla, 76
Thessalonica, *see* Salonike
Thyatira, 50
Tlos, 90
Trajan, emperor, 61

Tyre, in Phoenicia, 88, 90

Utica, 62

Valerian, emperor, 38, 43
Verus, Lucius, emperor, 93, 95, 96–8

Xanthos, 90
xustarchês, 51

Zeus, 16
Zeuxidemus Aristus Zeno, P. Aelius,
   94–5